"Ralph and Sajan capture the essence of the disruptive change underway across industries that requires a mindset shift in how we capture value. Understanding that an organization is part of a broader ecosystem that encompasses your related, as well as unrelated, industries as a source of innovation remains an untapped source of new value. The competitive firms of the immediate future will harness this mindset to their advantage, focusing less on 'must be built here' strategies.

"*Topple* provides a clear set of questions with directions on how to find the answers, along with examples of these guidelines being put into action. This is a much-needed, provocative, and welcome change from a typical business book with its well-structured format with multiple examples. *Topple* is a pragmatic guide to the what, when, and how aspects of executing, breaking down complex and often difficult topics in clear, concise language.

"A critical read for anyone or any organization expecting to stay competitive in the immediate future."

—DAN WOLLENBERG, Senior Vice President,
Transformation, JPMorgan Chase

"Many talk about the rise of business ecosystems as tomorrow's competitive strategy, but few have actually taken that journey and can provide pragmatic steps for how to do so. Ralph can and has. He has a unique capability to make you think differently and can guide you to take action as a result. The world has already changed. As an industry, we tend to be behind in how to take advantage of these changes. That's where *Topple* comes in. Read and act."

—MICHAEL CHAN, CEO, RHB Bank

"Working alongside Ralph with his prescient insight and pragmatic frameworks vitally challenged our way of thinking. Our business was headed for irrelevance. We needed this new approach. Navigating your company so that it is essential in its ecosystem is the only goal worth investing in; this book's insight and methodology take that imperative from the world of fuzzy concepts to the reality of execution."

—DYLAN GARNETT, CEO, Metropolitan Health

"Creating new growth is difficult. Finding new business models that create both greater economic value and societal benefit to support that new growth is critical. These are hard but necessary to do in the bio-tech and pharmaceutical worlds. Ecosystem-centric business models are the logical and the clear path forward to meeting these objectives. Ralph and Sajan challenge the status quo of how we typically think about new models of growth and customer engagement and provide a series of pragmatic steps to take advantage of them. A unique combination."

—DIRK SCHAPELER, Director of Life Science, iHub; Vice President, Digital Innovation, Bayer Pharma AG

"We fund a range of technology and disruptive companies in the renewable energy space globally. It's clear to us that new business models are rapidly emerging. These new business models are the key to explosive growth. Ralph and Sajan have written a powerful book on what makes these models work, but most importantly, they have done so in a pragmatic way, providing a 'field guide' of what type of business ecosystems are relevant for you, what roles you play within them, and how to think about your capabilities to do so. This is critical, particularly, as large companies struggle to drive explosive growth and work with start-ups and tech companies outside of any traditional industry boundary."

—ALEX O'CINNEADE, CEO, Founder, Gore Capital

"We work with top executives throughout the capital market and investment industries. There are few topics as important and urgent as figuring out new business models for distinctive and sustainable growth. Welborn and Pillai have their pulse on what these models are and how to take advantage of them for senior business executives. I cannot more strongly recommend making the time to, as they put it, 'make sense' and 'take action' on the clearly rapidly emerging new business models for growth."

—AL MELLINA, CEO, Managing Partner, Gartland & Mellina Group

"In 50 years, when we look back at the business landscape of the early 21st century, the criticality of ecosystem-centric business models will be self-evident. Companies that ask the right strategic questions now will be the ones that thrive in the future, and this book is literally ground zero in the boundary-blurring, industry-toppling, ecosystem-centric future of value creation for forward-thinking corporations."

—SCOTT COHEN, Cofounder, Innovation Leader

"Global public health represents a 'wicked problem' requiring different types of organizations to realize sustainable health outcomes. But, getting them to work together is extremely difficult, because they have their own objectives and priorities. Ralph has been working on similar types of wicked problems in other industries. His emphasis on what is common to these types of challenges and how to overcome them is extremely helpful. His description of the new competitive landscape that we find ourselves in and what to do about it is a refreshing new way to look at the challenges we face and how can we tackle them."

—GAIL CASSELL, MD, PhD, former President, Institute of Medicine, National Science Foundation, Harvard Medical School

"There's nothing harder today than driving business and technology transformation. Nearly everyone is working on it but most people are struggling. Welborn and Pillai explain why and what to do about it. There is a new competitive landscape everyone is facing that requires new approaches to capitalize on it and take advantage of the new transformation models it requires. What we've been doing before and what most are doing now won't work. *Topple* is an important book: provocative yet pragmatic at the same time."

—DAVE SANDERS, CEO, Dallas Advisory Group

"A tour-de-force of what may well be the most significant change in how we build and grow value in the 21st century! Insightful, powerful, and thought provoking, *Topple* will forever change the way you look at business."

—THOMAS KOULOPOULOS, Chairman, The Delphi Group

TOPPLE

The End of Firm-Based Strategy *and*
the Rise of New Models for Explosive Growth

TOPPLE

RALPH WELBORN, PhD
& SAJAN PILLAI

GREENLEAF
BOOK GROUP PRESS

This publication is designed to provide accurate and authoritative information in regard to the subject matter covered. It is sold with the understanding that the publisher and author are not engaged in rendering legal, accounting, or other professional services. If legal advice or other expert assistance is required, the services of a competent professional should be sought.

Published by Greenleaf Book Group Press
Austin, Texas
www.gbgpress.com

Distributed by Greenleaf Book Group

For ordering information or special discounts for bulk purchases, please contact Greenleaf Book Group at PO Box 91869, Austin, TX 78709, 512.891.6100.

Design and composition by Greenleaf Book Group
Cover design by Greenleaf Book Group
Cover images: ©iStockphoto.com/Nastco; ©iStockphoto.com/urfinguss; ©iStockphoto.com/PhonlamaiPhoto;

Publisher's Cataloging-in-Publication data is available.

Print ISBN: 978-1-62634-489-1

eBook ISBN: 978-1-62634-490-7

Part of the Tree Neutral® program, which offsets the number of trees consumed in the production and printing of this book by taking proactive steps, such as planting trees in direct proportion to the number of trees used: www.treeneutral.com

TreeNeutral

Printed in the United States of America on acid-free paper

18 19 20 21 22 23   10 9 8 7 6 5 4 3 2 1

First Edition

We build the road as we travel.

—*Antonio Machado*

Also by Ralph Welborn

Ralph Welborn has coauthored two previous books with a dear friend and colleague, Vince Kasten.

The Jericho Principle: How Companies Use Strategic Collaboration to Find New Sources of Value (John Wiley, 2003)

The Jericho Principle describes a range of emerging collaborative business models and capabilities to drive innovation and new sources of value.

Get It Done! A Blueprint for Business Execution (John Wiley, 2005)

Get It Done! focuses on how to bridge the gap between strategic objectives/intent and everyday execution. Executives and stakeholders within an organization often have different objectives. They certainly have different responsibilities and ways to get done what needs to get done. No wonder gaps often exist between strategic intent and what gets done. *Get It Done!* provides pragmatic lessons and frameworks drawn from transformation efforts around the world to bridge these gaps—respecting the different perspectives, personalities, and processes various leaders bring to the table and helping to align them to get done what needs to get done.

To Mom and Dad

Contents

Introduction

A new lens often highlights new objects to look at or helps us see old ones in new ways. Business ecosystems are such a lens. They are like the Hubble Telescope: you may be looking at the same skies, but with this new perspective you are able to see new stars and forces that connect them in ways you could never visualize before. If you look at your competitive landscape through the lens of business ecosystems, you begin to discover previously unseen elements, connections, and explosive growth opportunities, making visible what previously had been invisible.

Value seen is value captured. Looking at your new competitive landscape from an ecosystem perspective has two pragmatic benefits. First, it changes the vantage point of how you look at your competitive environments. One thing we all know: these environments are changing. Quickly. But there's one thing we often don't know: what to do about these changes. Broadening your perspective of the ecosystem in which you and your customers are engaged begins to provide a pragmatic appreciation for how changes have ripple effects—some easy to see and others impossible to predict—which helps you figure out what to do and how to do it.

Second, the blunt reality is that the explosive growth models of today and tomorrow are ecosystem-centric business ones. Consequently, figuring out what these new models are and how to take advantage of them is no longer a luxury but an imperative to take advantage of the new growth opportunities they catalyze.

We have had the privilege of working with bold leaders around the world to take advantage of market shifts they knew were coming. These leaders have two attributes in common, irrespective of industry, type of organization, or geography: First, their rigorous curiosity—continually seeking to understand shifts in technological advances, regulatory policy, customer expectations, and behavioral changes, and what these shifts might mean for their organizations. Second, their impatience—pushing them to move quickly to take advantage of opportunities in new ways.

New ways is the critical phrase here.

Many organizations continue to do what they've done before, only better-faster-cheaper. Or they invest in capabilities and technologies like and where everyone else does. Neither of these is a recipe for explosive growth.

What these bold leaders sought was insight into new models for distinctive, sustainable, and explosive growth. They recognized that there had to be lessons, insights, and models they could learn from and extend to capture new sources of value in new ways.

And there are. This book will focus on insights, lessons, and methods that take advantage of the explosive growth models that underlie the fundamental shifts in the competitive landscapes we all face.

Markets in the twentieth century followed certain patterns around scale and efficiency. Markets in the twenty-first century are reflecting their own—and different—patterns of value creation and growth. These differences reflect the extraordinarily dynamic environment many industries face, where the economics, customers, technologies, and sources of value are shifting from *economies of scale* to *economies of ecosystem engagement*. Ecosystem-centric business models are a logical reflection of these shifts and the new opportunities they create.

Our objective for this book is nothing less than to do for ecosystem-centric business models (new business models to capture explosive growth) what Jim Champy's *Reengineering the Corporation* did for reengineering (by focusing on process) and the Business Model Canvas has done for clarifying internal business capabilities (by aligning programs and messaging).

Admittedly this is an audacious goal. However, we live at an incredible time of shifting business models, with opportunities of extraordinary economic value and societal impact to be catalyzed and captured—if only we pay attention to how to do so. Change always creates new winners and losers, hence the imperative and resulting opportunities. We hope that after reading this book, you will be able to:

- Recognize the structural underpinnings of these shifts

- Begin to take advantage of them to capture new sources of value in new ways

- Realize that more of the same—the Red Queen's[1] race of running faster and faster but staying in the same competitive place—is no longer a winning strategy . . . if your objective is nonincremental, explosive growth

- Respond to the new opportunities that a shifting environment creates and new business models, powered by ecosystem-centric strategies

The Road Ahead

This book teases apart different threads of what we call *the new strategic questions* that underlie the explosive growth models powered by business ecosystems. Together they form a tapestry of new types of insight and point to a pragmatic method to execute your corporate strategy from an ecosystem perspective. Many of the examples and tools we describe are based on engagements we have personally led around the world in different industries.

Chapter 1 explains the need for a new set of strategic questions.

---

1   Character from *Through the Looking-Glass*, Lewis Carroll's sequel to *Alice's Adventures in Wonderland*.

The objectives of strategy and the competitive game played are straightforward: to identify and capture new sources of value in new ways. The explosive growth leaders of today lead us to new ways to play this game. These reveal lessons and insights to explore and also pragmatic steps to take that build upon them in new ways, given the inevitable adaptive shifts that technological advances, customer expectations, policy changes, and business model innovations always create. This chapter asks and answers the questions:

What is the new competitive landscape that we're all facing, and why are business ecosystems its underpinnings? What is the pragmatic definition and set of characteristics of a business ecosystem? And what is it about them that underlies so many of today's and tomorrow's explosive growth companies? Why, specifically, do all of these changes require a new set of strategic questions? And most importantly, what are these questions, and how do we begin to answer them to take advantage of the new growth opportunities that such changes always create?

New questions require new answers, with implications for creating value, engaging customers, developing capabilities, and shaping ecosystems—in new ways. The rest of the book explores these implications, providing examples, frameworks, lessons, and suggestions for how to do so, all in service of helping you make sense of them so you can take action differently on the explosive growth opportunities that make up the new competitive landscape.

Section 1 suggests a new framework of value from an ecosystem perspective. This matters. New business models rest on new methods of engagement—not only with customers but also with other actors within the ecosystem in which they and their customers engage. More often than not, these other actors come from other industries, bringing capabilities, insights, and different types of value that motivate their behavior. Figuring out how to orchestrate such differences toward a common objective depends on pragmatic insight into what motivates behavior, along with new methods to do so. All of this rests on a new framework, and language, of value.

Chapter 2 describes such a framework, and the key elements that make it useful and executable. It answers questions such as:

What are the distinctive foundations of value underlying our new competitive landscapes? How do we identify where value is being created and destroyed in our ecosystem? And how is that value being distributed across the new winners and losers, with what implications for whom to engage with, when, and how to do so?

A business ecosystem reflects a new business model based on orchestrating capabilities from different types of organizations to capture new sources of value. Clearly, different types of organizations (and even different stakeholders within any one organization) care about, or are motivated by, different types of value. *How can this work? How does this work? How do you orchestrate different types of stakeholders in a sustainable, effective manner?*

Chapter 3 answers these questions, peppered with examples and pragmatic frameworks underlying them.

Chapter 4 concludes this section with perspectives on how to size one's ecosystem. It explores questions such as:

What makes up our total ecosystem opportunity (TEO)? Given that insight, what parts of it should we focus on? And what are some of the structural considerations—the control points of value—that help determine the largest opportunities to unlock the TEO?

Discussions of value mean nothing unless we understand new ways to engage our customers, given our changed competitive landscapes. Fabled business strategist Peter Drucker once put it like this: no customers, no business. As we all well know, technologies advance, customer expectations change, and business models innovate. These are all interwoven, but the key thread holding them together is the center one—the customer—hence the focus and energy spent by many (most?) organizations on customer experience and the clarion call for customer centricity. Which all makes sense. Perhaps.

An ecosystem perspective shifts how we make sense of new opportunities ahead of us. It also challenges our current thinking about customer

experience and centricity and points to new ways to engage the customer—
if your objective is nonincremental, high-impact growth.

Section 2 explores new ways to engage your customers from an ecosystem perspective.

Chapter 5 suggests new ways to think about, and execute on, customer experience. Chapter 6 builds upon these perspectives and suggests how our current approach to customer centricity limits the type of
impact, and value, we can offer to customers—from their perspective—
and the ecosystems in which they spend their time, energy, and monies.

Spoiler alert. This section's description of how to engage customers
from an ecosystem perspective, in ways that matter to them, differs from
typical approaches. These new methods are complementary to the traditional approaches to journey mapping, customer segmentation, "magic
moments," and design thinking that motivate so much discussion around
customer engagement today, which is why the final chapter in this section, Chapter 6, is called "Beyond Customer Centricity to Ecosystem
Engagement." Specific questions this section answers include:

*How does an ecosystem perspective shift one's focus from any particular
set of products or services, firm, or customer to the ecosystem in which they all
engage? How does this shift help clarify specific (often counterintuitive) points
of market opportunity or customer friction to focus on? And how do we figure
out what the ecosystems are that customers engage in? How do we use that
insight to identify potential new sources of value that they care about and that
may have implications for the bundle of products, services, and experiences that
we may need/want to create to engage in those ecosystems?*

Reading books and describing examples are one thing. Knowing
how to apply their insights is often quite another. What we, the authors,
often want after reading a book or having a discussion is something akin
to a field guide, a how-to guide regarding how to use the insights suggested through specific examples described and models used. The final
section, Section 3, was written with this in mind.

All of the chapters are filled with examples, drawn from different
industries and geographies to illustrate specific points. The examples are

wrapped by models that elucidate, much like an X-ray, key implications of the topic. When, for example, we talk about engaging a customer from an ecosystem perspective, we provide both an example and models used to clarify not only *what* was done but more importantly *how* it was done.

Chapter 7 was written as a field guide to answer the new strategic questions. It comprises the how-to part of the book. It describes models we've found useful to answer those questions. It also illustrates how the models have been pieced together—Lego-block style—to support three common types of projects: digital transformation, new ways to engage one's customers, and getting more out of one's R&D and innovation portfolio. Other examples could have been used, but we selected these for a simple reason: they reflect hot topics of the day. We use them to show how models we discuss, and examples we use, can be pulled together for these and other types of projects you have.

Chapter 8, the final chapter, distills key lessons of the book. It concludes with a brief exploration of the implications of our new competitive landscape and the opportunities of business model innovation, powered by ecosystem business strategies, to catalyze explosive growth, as new ways to create both greater economic value and societal impact.

With Gratitude

There are many who have helped us see the patterns underlying these models as they began to form a decade ago and have helped us both design and deploy them. To all of you, we say thank you for helping us distill the lessons, insights, models, and frameworks that we share.

And to our readers, we hope that we provoke you to see your competitive environments differently, in a way that compels you to act with speed and scale to capture new sources of value in new ways. That's the challenge and the opportunity ahead of you.

1

The New Strategic Questions
for Explosive Growth

Disruption. The very word strikes disdain, despair, or delight into the heart of established businesses. Disdain because they believe "it can't happen to me—I'm one of the market leaders and know what to do." Despair because of what they see: Amazon versus the bookstore, Apple versus the cell phone, Uber versus the taxi, Tesla versus the energy industry, Tencent versus the media and payment industries, and many others to come. Delight because of the same, of what they see—and the opportunity to capture explosive new sources of value.

A Changed World Requires New Perspectives

Explosive growth has always, historically and across industries, come from tackling consumer friction (e.g., make it radically simple) or nonconsumption (e.g., bring new customers onto the field, in new ways). That's it. What has changed are the ease and speed of connectivity (free and everywhere), improved sense-making (formally known as insight and analytics, now as cognitive), and production technologies (exemplified by robotics and machine learning) that are uncovering these growth opportunities in every industry everywhere. Identifying and capturing these explosive opportunities requires a rethink and redo of what strategy is supposed to do—namely, clarify where to focus and, most importantly, how to execute.

The objective of the strategy and competitive game is straightforward: to identify and capture new sources of value in new ways. The capabilities to play are equally straightforward—if you know the rules and which capabilities to double down on. It is the rules—the questions and methods—underlying strategy that need to be reframed based on the new competitive landscapes we all face and the explosive (new) growth opportunities they catalyze.

The past forty years of corporate strategy have focused primarily on building firm-based competitive advantages to maintain or to improve growth. Strategic insight, positioning, and execution have all been variations on this focus. But times and technologies change, as do customer expectations and organizational responses that both reflect and drive these changes. The things that made many organizations successful up to now no longer will.

And here it gets interesting.

The most successful and explosive growth leaders—whether Tencent or Tesla, Amazon or Alibaba, Gilead or Google, Microsoft or Martin Marietta Materials, what Schneider Electric has done and what General Electric is trying to do—all reflect the new competitive reality:

The new competitive landscape will be shaped less by firm-specific strategies and more by new business models, powered by ecosystem-centric strategies.

There are new strategic questions in town. They underlie each of the companies mentioned above and are powering the ecosystem-centric business models they—and the many other explosive growth companies—reflect.

The questions are—

- Where is value being created and destroyed in the ecosystem you and your customers are engaged in?
- With that insight, how do you shape, influence, or just plain *fit* into that ecosystem to capture this value?
- What are the new capabilities critical to doing so?

Answers to these questions have significant implications for (a) new sources of value to capture; (b) new methods to engage your customers; (c) the new 20 percent of capabilities critical to doing so; and (d) novel business models to orchestrate them.

Why does this matter now? And why use this seemingly clumsy term, *business ecosystem*?

Because our competitive landscape has changed for good.

Doing More of the Same—Only Better, Faster, Cheaper— Is No Way to Drive Explosive Growth

Dylan Garnett is CEO of Metropolitan Health, Africa's largest health insurance third-party administrator.[2] Dylan, Metropolitan Health, and South Africa are at a policy and economic inflection point. South Africa has a population of approximately 52 million people. Eight million are covered by health insurance. The South African government is exploring options to provide health insurance for the balance of those without insurance, approximately 44 million people. The range of options regarding how to do so is broad—from nationalizing the health care system based on a one-payer model, such as in Canada and the United Kingdom, to creating multiple segmented insurance carriers that target different segments of the population. From a policy perspective, we don't know what specific steps will be taken. What we do know is that the way businesses are organized and what they do will change—dramatically. One thing is clear, as Dylan put it so eloquently, "Businesses are optimized for a world that no longer exists . . . and the environment that we structured our business around is transforming quickly, requiring fundamentally new ways to engage our customers, our stakeholders, and our markets."[3]

This is not an unusual story. It is one repeated throughout the world, across industries, irrespective of size. The logic of doing more of the same,

2   Dylan Garnett is now the former CEO of Metropolitan Health. At the time of our writing, he was CEO, which is why we use the present tense.

3   Discussion, October 2013.

only better-faster-cheaper, is not sustainable. Not for long. As quick proof points, merely observe—

- **Accelerating topple rates.** *Topple rate* is a fancy term for a simple observation: namely, the rate at which companies fall off or topple from the Fortune 500 or Global 2000 list is accelerating. Every year for the past twelve years, more than twenty companies toppled from the Fortune 500 list, reflecting a turnover of nearly 80 percent over the past twenty years. In addition, the average time spent on the Fortune 500 slipped down to fourteen years on average, from thirty-five years in 1970, and again is accelerating downward.

- **The market disproportionately rewards ecosystem-centric business models.** Explosive growth companies not only have higher growth rates but they carry much higher price-to-earnings ratios—five to ten times more—than similar-sized or other companies sharing their market focus but based on traditional business models.

What Are Business Ecosystems and Why Do They Matter?

Business ecosystems are methods of orchestrating capabilities from diverse organizations to capture new sources of value.

The explosive growth companies of tomorrow will be ecosystem-centric, but how they orchestrate different capabilities will differ. It is these differences that will make up the foundation of tomorrow's competitive advantage. These differences need to be where, what, and how strategy gets reframed and refocused, hence the criticality of the new strategic questions requiring deep insight into where value is being created and destroyed within your ecosystem, and what you do about it.

In a world of competing business ecosystems, the traditional methods of assessing competitive advantage and delivering strategic insight have become increasingly irrelevant. Many firms will continue to pursue traditional sources of advantage. They, however, will be increasingly vulnerable to disruption from competitors based on business model innovation, powered by ecosystem-centric strategies. This strategy boils down to identifying white space to fill (via tackling friction or nonconsumption, from a customer's perspective) and orchestrating capabilities from different actors to fill it. This is no minor change; it has significant impacts on—

- Customers to engage (in new ways)
- (New sources of) value to capture
- (New) capabilities to develop
- (New) business models to exploit
- Ecosystems to shape

Business ecosystems catalyze new ways to deliver value to your customers, stakeholders, and markets within the new competitive environment in which we all currently, and will increasingly, engage.

Business ecosystems are no aberration, nor are they a surprise. They reflect a natural, adaptive response to changes in the types of value that folks care about. They also illustrate the types of market friction or breakdown that can now be tackled, thanks to the new capabilities—and perspectives—catalyzed by technology innovation, behavioral expectations, regulatory changes, and novel business models.

Outlines of the New Approach

It's become a cliché: the Internet changes everything. In the world of corporate strategy, practitioners have looked deeply at how this change affects many activities—from product design to customer engagement, supply chains to value chains, digitization to transformation, marketing to production, and so on.

However, folks have yet to recognize the full impact of these and other changes on the focus and tools of strategic analysis that guide decision making. Traditional models of firm-based and industry-focused strategic insight must now be revised to account for disruptive change in five key elements of corporate strategy:

- **Unit of Focus.** Focus will shift from individual firms, products, or services to the different types of ecosystems that organizations and their customers engage in.

- **New Foundations of Value.** Foundations of value will shift from managing buyers, suppliers, entrants, substitutes, and rivals in order to squeeze more out of a given industry (i.e., traditional characteristics of industry attractiveness) to "owning" specific customer problems or market opportunities while orchestrating capabilities and shaping ecosystems to do so. These new foundations of value will stretch across traditional industry lines and require the design and execution of new methods to share risks and rewards across a wide range of organizations.

- **Competitive Advantage.** Competitive advantage will shift from seeking market differentiation based on a specific product or service to orchestrating capabilities from a diverse set of actors around the new foundations of value and specific parts of one's value chain.

- **The New 20 Percent.** The core capabilities that made you successful yesterday and today will be different from those you will need tomorrow.

- **Customer Engagement.** Organizations will move beyond traditional concepts of customer centricity: from seeking to delight customers or create magic moments (as the jargon and the current thinking about customer experience, design thinking, and journey mapping suggests) to figuring out where and how to engage customers in the ecosystems in which they're engaged, based on where *they spend* their time, money, and energy.

The outlines of this new model have been emerging for a decade in the likes of Tesla, Amazon, Tencent, Alibaba, and other explosive growth companies. But the model's implications for virtually every industry and firm remain poorly understood. The once-powerful model of managing owned and purchased resources to deliver value to a predefined customer is giving way to *clusters of firms* that plant a flag on specific sets of customer needs and orchestrate a range of capabilities from a diverse network of providers to meet them. *This* is different, a difference with staggering consequences, requiring moving from a better-faster-cheaper mind-set to one relentlessly focused on new ways to define value, engage customers, and orchestrate capabilities across industry and market boundaries.

Answering the new strategic questions involves a two-step process. The first step involves clarity about what makes up high-impact or potentially explosive growth opportunities—requiring an ecosystem perspective. The second step builds on that clarity to frame a new business model that moves you from (novel) insight to impact, with speed and scale (which requires methods to shape that ecosystem).

To paraphrase what the great Russian novelist Leo Tolstoy said about families, business ecosystems are similar, but they are similar in unique ways. Insight into what is different among them helps you—

- Identify where to focus—around new sources of potential value
- Clarify the critical new capabilities needed to capture that value
- Frame out different types of business model innovations, powered by ecosystem-centric strategies
- Articulate what roles need to be performed in those ecosystems, and figure out how to mobilize different types of stakeholders to do so

An ecosystem perspective catalyzes new ways to identify and capture new sources of value rather than merely extending your existing sources or markets. This perspective also opens up new choices to make about how to do so. At Metropolitan Health, Dylan Garnett faced a broad range of questions about how to engage the fundamental transformation he and millions of others experienced during the ongoing health system transformation. We will continue to check in with Dylan throughout the book to see how his ecosystem perspective opened up new doorways of opportunities he could walk through.

But first, we need to provide some frameworks and examples to make business ecosystems tangible, the first step to being able to answer the new strategic questions pragmatically. As Dave Brooks, the CEO of Unifrax, put it in one of our workshops around these topics, "Make [the concept] real, but make me think while you are doing so."

What's Similar?

While different types of business ecosystems exist, they all share three underlying similarities.

First—Unit of Focus

As discussed earlier, many leaders take their own department, organization, firm, or business as their point of focus, seeking to optimize the performance of that particular unit. A key assumption of this focus is that it is sufficient to maximize the performance of one's firm (or organization) vis-à-vis other firms. "Take care of yourself" and seek to grow and take market share from others within your industry. This seems logical enough and has been demonstrably effective for the past hundred years. Much of the training in business school and management experience has been based on *taking the firm as the primary unit of focus*. This focus has worked well in the world of clearly defined industry classifications and market boundaries.

However, a changed world has given rise to new ways to engage customers and markets that require shifts in the strategic questions we ask and the execution steps we take. Shifting the unit of focus from *the firm* to *the ecosystem in which you and your customers engage* provides a new perspective on where to focus and how to do so.

Many (most?) explosive growth opportunities are, to use a hackneyed phrase, *convergence plays*. Simply, *convergence* refers to activities from different industries that combine together, or converge, to meet a specific need. M-Pesa, Safaricom's rapidly growing business in mobile money, has become a classic example of such a convergence play. M-Pesa's platform handles approximately 33 percent of Kenya's GDP financial transactional value through its mobile network today.

M-Pesa facilitates commerce, fusing the remittance and payment functions of a bank with the immediacy and reach of a telecommunications carrier. It enables social connectivity as well, through the provisioning and distribution of its airtime minutes as mechanisms of barter, social exchange, and community building. M-Pesa has created a new *currency of exchange*—fusing financial, commerce, and social strengthening capabilities.

M-Pesa is but one of a number of examples that could be cited to illustrate convergence plays. Others exist at the intersections of health and wealth, nano-credit and mobile access, music distribution and community building; even the automobile industry has gotten into the act.[4] Without exception, all of the US-headquartered automobile companies now consider themselves to be mobility rather than transportation companies, declaring themselves such at the 2015 annual Detroit Automobile Show.

A number of businesses have been left behind in convergence plays. Merely look at who the explosive entrepreneurs are and the difficult-to-launch-and-even-more-difficult-to-sustain attempts at capturing some of these convergent business areas by (typically) established businesses.

Many reasons account for this difficulty. But the one to highlight is the difficulty that many companies have seeing the ecosystem in which they are embedded as a source of shifting value. Instead, they tend to optimize what they have done before—to protect the assets and services that drove their growth in the first place. With pressures on ongoing profitability, they seek to tighten down the operational hatches, squeeze out operational costs, and protect their declining margins as long as possible.

---

4   See William Eggers and Paul Macmillan, *The Solution Revolution* (Boston: Harvard Business Review Press, 2013) for more examples.

A common instinct is to "do more faster with less and cheaper." Organizational attempts at *doing new* tend to rub against the rails of how "things have always been done" or move too slowly because they are constrained by the industry logic and business systems that once made them great.

An ecosystem perspective looks at the question of where value is being created and destroyed within a changing competitive environment and customer-needs perspectives, irrespective of what individual actors are doing. It provides insight into systemic shifts of economic opportunity and, critically, into the new foundations of capabilities, assets, and activities that need to be brought together to capture those new sources of value—industry boundaries be damned. Since when does a customer care who meets their needs, as long as they are met in a way that is affordable and relevant?

The key point here is simple: many of our explosive growth opportunities are convergence plays. Convergence plays require taking an ecosystem perspective. This perspective allows you to see how, where, and by whom value is being created and destroyed. By so doing, it helps you identify new foundations of value critical to capturing new sources of growth that an ecosystem perspective exposes. It also logically leads us to the next similarity across the business models.

Second—Asking and Answering the New Strategic Questions

Tomorrow's competitive environment will be shaped by ecosystem-centric business models. Just look at the "picking sides" process involved in Google's Android versus Apple's iOS; Walmart versus Amazon and their attempts to *lock-in* their suppliers and partners with both carrots and sticks, depending on choices they make regarding who they support; or the giant battles among Google, Facebook, Apple, and, increasingly relevant again, Microsoft in platforms of social engagement.

Satya Nadella, Microsoft's CEO, has well recognized the imperative to change how Microsoft engages in the consumer and business ecosystems, being responsive to the collective voice they reflect rather than being dictated to by any one particular firm, even one as large as Microsoft. His shift in how Microsoft engages, moving from closed to increasingly open, is the crisp lesson of a firm recognizing that it was optimized for a world that no longer exists and needs new ways to engage its customers, stakeholders, and markets in order to capture new and emerging sources of value. Microsoft used to be the grand master of ecosystem strategy but lost its way during the past ten years. Nadella is attempting to rearchitect Microsoft's ecosystem, recognizing that "value in ecosystems stems from being able to control the points of leverage . . . which requires us to be able to work across any platform, even those controlled by competitors."[5]

Why new strategic questions? What's the matter with the ones we've been using for years? Shifting your focus toward the ecosystem you are engaged in creates the possibility of seeing a new set of interactions, pressures, challenges, and opportunities that you couldn't see before. You see different things if you're looking out a window from the fiftieth floor than one on the first floor. This doesn't mean that what you see and the questions you ask are any less important. But it does mean that the questions asked from a different perspective provide a broader context and canvas from which you can see new potential opportunities.

There are three questions that structure many strategic directions. Variants of these exist, of course. But at their core they reflect the same three questions:

- Where do we make money?

- Where and how can we cut costs?

- How do we shape the market perception of our value proposition?

These are fine operational questions, critical to ensuring that your execution plan is well thought through. But they are certainly no longer the starting set of questions to answer for any effective growth strategy. The new strategic questions are—

---

5   Jessi Hempel, "Restart, Microsoft in the Age of Satya Nadella," *Wired*, Feb. 2015, accessed Dec. 16, 2015, http://www.wired.com/2015/01/microsoft-nadella/.

- Where is value being created and destroyed in the ecosystem in which you and your customers are engaged?

- How do we shape, influence, or just plain *fit* into that ecosystem to capture this value?

- What are the new capabilities and underlying new business models needed to do so?

Let's look at an example of the shift from the traditional to the new strategic questions.

Unifrax is a privately held market leader in a highly technical market. They manufacture specialized fibers to support thermal insulation and emission controls, providing an Intel-Inside-like value to some of the critical infrastructure industries globally, such as energy, transportation, and construction. They have been growing at a healthy clip for years and, given their quality and market structure, have had a consistently rich margin and global growth record. According to Dave, their former CEO, this was not enough. He sought models for nonincremental growth. He expressed frustration with the many strategy firms that had come through his office over the years, seeking to work with him. They all asked variants of the traditional three questions mentioned above. They told him that they could help him through asking and answering, "Where did he think he might expand his market, with what products? Where and how did he think they could expand while increasing productivity per employee? And how did he think he could sell more to existing and new customers?" These were but slight variants of the traditional questions, and per Dave, something his team dealt quite well with every day. As he put it, these were important operational rather than strategic questions; they "provide[d] no insight into how to dramatically drive new types of growth."

On the other hand, Dave was struck by these questions: *Where is value being created and destroyed in your ecosystem? How do you shape it to capture new and distinctive sources of value?* Dave said, "This is provocative and reframes how we look at the market, who we engage with, and novel ways to do so."[6]

We've already mentioned that explosive growth across industries and history comes from tackling consumer friction or nonconsumption. In less jargony terms, it comes from solving specific customer or market problems or meeting specific needs—from their perspective, based on where they spend their time, energy, and resources. This is quite different from the traditional questions that seek to expand what you already have, searching for so-called market white space or opportunities to sell more of what you already do and deliver what you already make. They start from within your organizational walls, search outward, and march into that space based on the kit of products and services you already have.

The new strategic questions start from a different vantage point. They start from outside your organizational walls, distilling what specific market or customer friction points there are or where nonconsumption exists. Figuring out how to meet these needs typically requires capabilities, products, and services beyond what any one particular firm—or even industry—can bring to the table.

Stated differently, *the new strategic questions start with a crisp articulation of needs and then frame what capabilities are needed to meet them.* They prompt you to look for organizations, typically a combination of them, that can provide those capabilities, irrespective of industry, and then figure out how to orchestrate them in service of those needs.

Let's take an example. (Note: we draw the next couple of examples from Africa for two simple reasons. First, not as many people know of these specific examples, enabling them to bring an openness to their description and the lessons they suggest. Second, to highlight the profound similarity underlying these models, irrespective of industry and geography.)

Millions of people in East and West Africa make no more than two dollars a day. The following is a typical challenge facing many of these people. Someone runs out of money on, say, Tuesday, and lacks the

---

6 Interview, December 12, 2015.

capability to buy milk for their family until they get paid again in a few days, say Friday. The question becomes, How do you provide a product or service that allows them to obtain food before they have money available?

The story of two different firms and their efforts to tackle this problem illustrates the difference between the traditional strategic questions and ecosystem-centric ones, and how they led to extremely different operational responses and market impact.

Equity Bank is one of Africa's fastest-growing banks with significant presence throughout West and East Africa. They defined this problem as one of needing to create micro-loan capabilities. They saw what many did: namely, that well over 160 million people who make less than two dollars a day in Kenya and Nigeria faced this problem. This was a clear market opportunity, if they could march into that space. Doing so required them to dramatically reduce the costs of both providing and servicing these loans through their existing and vast distribution channels—namely, correspondent banks and agents. The steps they took to do this included looking at their existing loan portfolio, trimming back on the features that made up their loan products, and then figuring out how (a) they could take costs out of their distribution and sales network and (b) train their agents to sell the benefit of these modified products to those who previously had no access to them. After trial and error in getting costs down to support a reasonable risk/return ratio, they were able to get to a steady state of selling a certain number of these payday loans per month. Not bad.

MoDe, a start-up out of Kenya, cofounded by executives from the global bank HSBC, started from a different perspective. They defined the market need differently than did Equity Bank. The business problem was not couched as an opportunity to sell cheaper payday loans but rather as a specific challenge for low-income people to obtain critical items for their family—of access to critical goods to purchase and the capability to acquire them without the use of cash. The challenge was defined as a market breakdown; the traditional economics could not work to provide low-cost products. Few banks would enter this market, and even if they did, not nearly enough people could consume the products offered. Defining the problem this way—as one of nonconsumption (people could not afford to purchase critical items) and market failure (reflecting the difficulty in getting the loans to the people who needed them in different parts of the region where there weren't distribution channels)—set the team on an ecosystem-centric path.

Starting with an *outside-in* perspective around market needs led the team to reframe the challenge around *access* and *acquiring* goods and the capabilities needed to overcome those challenges through orchestrating capabilities from different types of organizations. The capabilities needed to support access, for example, become clear quickly. One thing West and East Africa have lots of is cell phones.[7] Well over 300 million mobile phones are distributed throughout a population of approximately 225 million in Kenya and Nigeria, averaging 1.3 phones per person.

So, for the executive team, building a relationship with Kenya's major telecom provider—Safaricom—became critical for two reasons. First, access. Phones are critical touchpoints for nearly everyone: customers and businesses. With them you can figure out who has the type of goods you need to buy. Second, medium of exchange. Mobile phones have mobile minutes on them. Mobile minutes are a form of exchange—of value—that can be transferred to other parties, whether as gifts or as forms of payment for goods. Customers who did not have money to pay for goods—the use case and new market opportunity—could pay for goods with mobile minutes rather than with cash. This was a breakthrough insight, one built on rethinking the fundamental market problem they needed to solve and consequently designing the new capabilities critical to doing so. Access to the switch data of Safaricom for insight on who had which goods to acquire, and the use of mobile minutes as a new medium of exchange—rather than being constrained by having to use cash—were the breakthroughs needed to capture a rich source of new value and growth. Figuring out how to orchestrate these capabilities from

---

7 "Cellphones in Africa: Communication Lifeline," Pew Research Center, April 15, 2015, http://www.pewglobal.org/2015/04/15/cell-phones-in-africa-communication-lifeline/.

different organizations became, then, the next critical step to getting this from strategic insight to market impact.

MoDe developed an extremely simple text-based (since the majority of these 300+ million phones were not visually rich smartphones) application that enabled people to get mechanisms of exchange immediately wherever they were, ones that could be repaid when they "topped up"— or renewed their mobile minutes. The problem of access was eliminated. You required no correspondent bank or agents; distribution was handled by the ubiquitous mobile phone. The costs of delivering and servicing the product plummeted to nearly zero, since everything was delivered wirelessly, 80 percent less than what it cost Equity Bank to provide. The upshot? While Equity Bank was doing a certain number of loans per month, MoDe was providing that same number per week.

The extraordinary difference in performance resulted from starting with three directionally different strategic questions: How can we do more with what we already do (Equity Bank, an inside-out perspective)? What is a specific market need (whether from market breakdown and/or nonconsumption), and how do we orchestrate a wide range of capabilities to meet it (MoDe, an outside-in perspective)?

The new strategic questions focus on where new sources of value can be explored within the ecosystem of a specific market need. In our example, the need was *not* to sell more loans. The need was to provide access to some mechanism of exchange. Here, mobile minutes served as a proxy for funds, enabling people to do what they needed to do when they needed to do it. This is similar to Clayton Christensen's *jobs to be done* concept, whereby sources of value stem from looking at folks in terms of the jobs they care about and figuring out how to orchestrate the capabilities needed to get those jobs done.[8] The customer doesn't care where the capabilities come from. They have a need, and whoever can help them meet that need is the one they'll choose to do business with. Bill Gates years ago stated, "We need

8 Clayton M. Christensen, *The Innovator's Dilemma: The Revolutionary Book That Will Change the Way You Do Business* (Boston: Harvard Business Review Press, 1997).

banking, not banks." Providing access to some form of exchange—e.g., mobile minutes, micro-loans—does not depend on the traditional capabilities of a bank. And, clearly, as is well evidenced by the explosion of new ventures, investments, and technologies within the mobile payments space, the capabilities to meet the needs of funding—however, whenever, and wherever you want them—are coming quickly from lots of different firms other than just banks.[9]

Doing more of the same, only better-faster-cheaper (sound familiar?) makes capturing explosive and differentiated growth, simply put, hard. Kindly reflect on the lessons of the topple rates to ask yourself how prevalent this challenge is. Or ask yourself about the prevalence of the Red Queen, the nemesis of Lewis Carroll's Alice in Wonderland, mentioned earlier, who runs faster and faster but stays in the same place.

We have found the Red Queen to be an apt characterization of many businesses and leaders who seek to run harder and harder—whether through doing more with less or investing more and more but in ways similar to their competitors, which, to no surprise, tends to keep everyone in the same relative competitive position over time. We have started out many discussions about this queen with companies around the world. No matter the industry or geography, her very mention triggers wry smiles, grimaces, or sage nods regarding the relevance of her message to many businesses. How sustainable is the effort to try to continuously do more—better, faster, cheaper? The race to outexecute other people is a tough race to keep running. Just look at the topple rate numbers. Just look at your traditional (and new) competitors. Just ask Equity Bank.

The new strategic questions help make new sources of value visible. They also help to distill the third similarity underlying ecosystem-centric business models.

---

9   Discussion with David Sanders, founder of Dallas Advisory Partners and CEO of several start-ups, including a mobile payments firm, December 2016.

Third—Business Model Innovation

Businesses are optimized for a world that no longer exists. What made them successful yesterday will not be what makes them effective tomorrow. Many recognize this. The challenges are what to do and how to do it. As markets, regulations, customer expectations, and technologies change, so too do the capabilities needed to respond effectively to them. This is why business model innovation has become so critical and why so much attention is being paid to being agile and able to adapt with speed and scale to whatever the future will bring.

Many are facing a massive irony. While many well recognize both the urgency and criticality of new business models, many (most?) of their efforts are looking in all the wrong places. It's like the classic joke about the person looking for her lost car keys under a lamppost, even though she knows they're not there. "Why are you looking there," asks a bystander, "since you know your keys aren't there?" The seeker responds, "Because the light's better here." This is the Red Queen irony, writ large, and one that today's and tomorrow's explosive growth companies have taken to heart—to stop running this race and to ask, and answer, the new strategic questions in a way that looks in new areas to capture new sources of explosive growth in new ways. Doing so requires a business model: to figure out where to focus, how to focus, and how to execute with speed and scale.

Why Do This Discussion and This Topic Matter Now?

Ecosystem-centric business models are here to stay. How companies decide to engage with them will impact their long-term viability. There are four reasons this topic matters now.

I. The Center Cannot Hold

We are at the beginning of an irrevocable new model of economic value creation. But what remains poorly understood are the implications of this change for every other industry and firm. The old model of managing owned and purchased resources to deliver value to a predefined customer is giving way. In its place are models that feature clusters of firms that plant a flag on specific sets of customer needs and orchestrate a network of providers to meet them. The result? The emergence of a new competitive landscape that will be framed less by industry giants than by ecosystem-centric business models.

2. Opportunities Exist for Everyone to Capture New Sources of Value in New Ways

Of course, Apple has planted itself at the center of the mobile ecosystem, just as Google has done for information delivery, Facebook for community, and Amazon for radical simplicity to acquire anything. Based on these examples, it is tempting to conclude that the opportunities to lead an ecosystem, own its orchestration platform, and reap the resulting benefits are relatively few. But, in reality, the dynamics that drove their opportunities and the ecosystem-centric business models they designed to capture them are available to everyone.

3. New Winners and Losers Will Emerge

Change always creates new winners and losers. On the losing side, look at the accelerating topple rate, the turnover of nearly 80 percent over the past twenty years alone on the Fortune 500 list, with the average time spent on it down from thirty-five years to fourteen on average—and accelerating downward. On the winner side, look at the growth records and price-to-earnings ratios of ecosystem-centric businesses, multiples of traditional business models.

Not everyone will be the new Amazon, Google, or even the next unicorn, those companies that grow to more than $1 billion in valuation in short order. That is as unrealistic as it is unnecessary. Questions become, What lessons do we take from ecosystem-centric business models? Which do we keep? Which do we discard? Which type of business ecosystem is relevant for us? What role do we play within them, what capabilities do we bring to the table to do so, and how do we transform our business model to orchestrate them? And most importantly, what are the specific customer and market frictions or problems of nonconsumption to tackle, around which to focus this set of questions? These are the key questions to answer to drive nonincremental, explosive growth.

4. Products, Services, and Experiences Will Blur

Kevin Kelly cleverly characterizes this topic of blurring as the *liquidity* among products, services, and experiences.[10] Ask yourself a question: What product companies are not seeking to create services to protect, if not expand, the value of their products? And what service companies are not seeking to productize more of what they do for the same reason? Both types of companies seek to create an effective balance among products, services, and customer experience that extends their relevance and value opportunities. Organizations across all industry lines and countries are wrestling with what this (more) effective balance should be—and the implications of this balance, or liquidity, on what they do, how they do it, and with whom they do so.

New rules—new ways of making sense and taking action—are needed. We are providing a structured way to help folks use a new language to guide them through the new competitive landscape based on the new strategic questions.

So, questions for the reader don't start with, "Should we be part of a business ecosystem?" But rather, "Which type of business ecosystem is right for our business? How do we engage differently with our customers, stakeholders, and markets? With what implications? And what will be our new 20 percent of capabilities that will drive 70 percent of our value tomorrow, compared with those for today?"

---

10   Kevin Kelly, *The Inevitable: Understanding the 12 Technological Forces That Will Shape Our Future* (New York: Viking, 2016).

Value Seen Is Value Captured

If you can't see the sources of new, potentially explosive value—because you look for what you have always looked for based on what you've always done—then you will never be able to capture it. After all, it is impossible to go after what you can't see. Changing the focus from a department, a function, a business, or even an industry to that of an ecosystem automatically shifts your perspective of what you see and consequently where you focus. Seeing opportunities that others don't creates an opportunity for explosive growth. That's what this book is about. And that's what we begin to explore in the next section.

Building a New Language of Value, and Why It Matters

Mark, CEO of one of the world's largest sporting goods firms, was fielding questions on an investor call regarding the amount of investment his company was putting into different types of innovation, particularly on what it calls *big-based innovation*—breakthrough innovations designed to create new lines of business greater than $500 million a year. "When will the company get a return on its big investments?" Mark was asked. "I'll get back to you on that question" was his response—a response that triggered a flurry of internal activity to figure out the answer. The journey to answer it exposed rich and robust ways to build a new language about the various kinds of value they hoped to create throughout the ecosystem they were shaping, and a refined set of actions to capture that value.

Questions Are Hard

Ask a different question, get a different answer. This is an adage many of us heard from our teachers, if not parents or friends. We certainly did. One of us had an uncle who was a tenured professor of computer science and economics at Notre Dame. He used to prod his students and family to "see differently by asking different types of questions that few think to ask." Questions are hard. New types of questions are even harder. It's typically much easier simply to ask what many in our professions, and our businesses, have asked before. A risk of doing so, of course, stems from seeing what everyone else sees. New sources of value and explosive growth come from seeing and executing on what few others see and even fewer act on, all of which rests on asking new types of questions.

An ecosystem perspective changes the unit of focus from any one business, or even industry, to the network of interactions and actors in which we are all engaged. It only logically follows that many of the key terms—or questions—examined through a traditional lens expand when we look at them from an ecosystem-centric one. The notion of value is no different. What it is, how to measure it, and most importantly how a broader understanding of value, from an ecosystem perspective, impacts the way different types of organizations work together—this is what is different and is what Mark's example illustrates.

"When will we be net cash positive on the big investments we are making?" That was the starting question for Mark's direct reports—the president of new business, head of innovation, and the head of research and development. This was a fine, understandable question, just not the most effective one, given what they wanted to do—namely catalyze explosive growth as measured by a large new revenue stream based on foundational new capabilities.

No one, of course, can know with any certainty what will happen in the future. However, we can begin to figure out how to adapt to (a conservative approach) or help to shape (a bolder one) whatever future comes to pass. Clearly this is not something we can do alone. The world and our competitive environment are far too messy and involve way too many different actors, organizations, and tapestries of interactions to control. But we can influence them in a way that catalyzes and captures new sources of value. Changing one's unit of focus away from any one business, or even industry, to the broader ecosystem is a start toward influencing that tapestry of interactions. It raises new questions to ask and thereby creates new opportunities to pursue. It also suggests how and why Mark's question of "when will we be net cash positive?" had to change. We will return to this example throughout this section to describe how it did so and the implications that change had on catalyzing explosive growth, based on redefining value from an ecosystem perspective.

Section Road Map

Ecosystem-centric business models are built on a new framework of value. There is a set of elements key to turning this framework into pragmatic action to identify, yes, but more importantly to capture the new sources of value. The chapters in this section will describe and explore each of these elements using examples, models, and lessons to help you use the framework to guide action.

Chapter 2 will explore new foundations of value and their impact on who you are and what you do. As markets change, what worked for us before no longer will. Changes require new areas to focus on (what we call *new foundations of value*) and new capabilities (what we call *the new 20 percent*) to develop. Aside from these concepts, Chapter 2 will introduce one called *capabilities decay rate* or *half-life*—a framework extremely useful to gaining insight into the ongoing relevance of those capabilities that will drive (and have driven) the majority of your future (and previous) value.

It's one thing to know that an ecosystem-centric business model is critical to capturing explosive value. It's another to know how to orchestrate it. Chapter 3 introduces the concept of currencies and explores the use of shared value frameworks to support such orchestration. It provides a structured way both to get insight into what motivates different types of stakeholders and how to structure programs to keep them aligned—and focused.

Chapter 4 explores what we call TEO—total ecosystem opportunity— a pragmatic framework to assess both the economic and societal value around an ecosystem-driven opportunity. It also explores the implications of assessing TEO on whom to engage and why to do so.

The objective of this section is to build a new framework of ecosystem-centric value. With that in mind, let's get started.

2

New Foundations of Value—
Because the World Has Changed

Businesses have evolved—and honed—a set of core capabilities (some call them *competencies*) to meet the expectations of their customers, stakeholders, and markets. There has been an explosion of organizational effort over the past twenty years to identify one's core capabilities and figure out how to strengthen them. Approximately 20 percent of these core capabilities drive 70 percent of your total asset value delivered today. However, markets change, as do customer expectations. Consequently, it makes sense that a new 20 percent of capabilities will be critical for capturing new sources of value. And that's what we've found.

The New 20 Percent
There is a decay rate—or half-life—of the competitive relevance of an organization's capabilities. Stated differently, the value of any product or service and the capabilities underlying it (skill sets, software, distribution channel, customer relationship, media channels, or process) tend to lessen over time. Bluntly, they have been decaying at an accelerating rate over the past twenty years. No surprise. Technologies change, as do customer expectations and market dynamics, creating pressures (and opportunities) about

what to do and how to do it. The competitive half-life of products, services, skill sets, processes, and strategies is decreasing—with competition and the acceleration of change increasing. This observation tends to be of little, if any, surprise to anyone.

The idea of the new 20 percent, however, does tend to be a surprise.

The point is simple: there is a new 20 percent—a different 20 percent of capabilities critical to capturing 70 percent of new sources of value. Look at the example of MoDe vs. Equity Bank and the very different capabilities required to capture the new source of value they both sought. Who would have thought that competencies around analyzing switch data from telecom providers and the use of mobile minutes as a new form of exchange would be critical in order to acquire new sources of value in a way that benefited both the existing telecom provider and the new high-growth company? Clearly, in retrospect, it all makes sense. But it didn't before the value was seen and captured in new ways.

The same holds for all of the new sources of value from an ecosystem perspective.

Take Uber or Airbnb, two oft-cited examples of wildly successful companies that not only created new sources of value but also reflected new business models—ecosystem-centric ones—to do so.

Neither owns the capital assets that support their business: modes of transportation (cars, vans, helicopters) or lodging assets. The value of both lies in how they orchestrate different capabilities from the different actors within their ecosystems to address specific customer needs. For Uber, this includes mobile connectivity (from carriers), payment transactions (from banks or credit card companies), and modes of transportation (from owners). For Airbnb, swap out modes of transportation for types of lodging and you get a similar business model. Both of these—

- Are centered around what the customer wants to do
- Take friction out of what it is they want to do, making the service extraordinarily convenient

- Orchestrate different capabilities from different types of actors and organizations to meet these needs
- Rely on specific capabilities to enable that orchestration—their new 20 percent that drives their explosive growth model

These two companies from the so-called sharing economy are crisp examples of the prevalence and power of business ecosystems, and they're the reason it's important to figure out what new 20 percent of capabilities are needed in order to capture new sources of growth. Finding this answer is not a "nice-to-have" but an "imperative-to-do."

As is well known, the sharing economy encompasses a wide range of activities. It is built around a simple proposition: increase the use of human or physical resources orchestrated by an online platform or marketplace. Uber and its competitor Lyft have transformed private cars into common resources; Airbnb allows individuals to share their homes. Dozens of other shareable assets are forming to meet specific needs with a focus on taking out friction in day-to-day activities while creating new sources of value for the firms that orchestrate them *and* those whose assets are being shared. In 2013, revenues passing through the sharing economy into people's wallets were estimated to have exceeded $3.5 billion in the US, up 25 percent from the previous year. Airbnb has exceeded 10 million of what they call *guest-stays* since its 2008 launch, and as of mid-2017 it had more than 3 million properties listed. Meanwhile Uber claims to be doubling its revenue every four months.

A 2015 analysis out of Harvard's Shorenstein Center estimated that a 1 percent increase in Airbnb listings in Texas resulted in a 0.05 percent decrease in quarterly hotel revenues, an estimate compounded by Airbnb's rapid growth. It found that the impacts were "distributed unevenly across the industry, with lower-end hotels and hotels not catering to business travelers being the most affected."[11] Increasing reports regarding Uber and

---

11   Joanna Penn and John Wihbey, "Uber, Airbnb and Consequences of the Sharing Economy," Journalist's Resource, accessed Sept. 10, 2017, https://journalistsresource.org/studies/economics/business/airbnb-lyft -uber-bike-share-sharing-economy-research-roundup.

some of the local regulatory pressures against them stem from concerns that existing taxi and town car companies have about these new companies creating an unfair competitive environment. The dramatic fall in the price of taxicab medallions (a city-issued license permitting one to drive in a specific area) in New York City from well over $1 million per medallion to under $241,000, from 2014 to 2017, is but one example of the challenges and loss of value to the traditional players.[12] In addition, a number of reports are exploring to what extent the economic benefits accruing to those who orchestrate these sharing economy ecosystems are being "sufficiently" shared with those who drive or actually share their homes. This is a space to watch, with a specific consideration that a new 20 percent of capability underlies this new ecosystem that—

- Catalyzes the capture of new sources of value
- Serves as the control point around which other capabilities—assets, resources—are orchestrated from different actors who are docking into the ecosystem to capture part of the new value

Another consideration to note is that no company has *all* of the capabilities required to capture new sources of value. MoDe didn't own the switch data or mobile minutes critical to meeting the market need. Climate Corporation doesn't own the satellite transmission data critical to monitoring farmland centimeter by centimeter. Uber doesn't own the modes of transportation it orchestrates. However, they were the first to identify the types of capabilities—the new 20 percent—critical to capturing explosive new sources of growth and the business model needed to orchestrate them all.

There are three points to consider around the concept of the new 20 percent:

- Explosive growth comes from tackling market/consumer friction and/or nonconsumption.

---

12   "The Taxi King," *Planet Money*, NPR, Episode 643, July 31, 2015, http://www.npr.org/sections/money/2015/07/31/428157211/episode-643-the-taxi-king.

- There will be a new 20 percent of capabilities critical to capturing 70 percent of the new value underlying that growth.

- Figuring out *how* to orchestrate these capabilities across diverse actors to capture the new sources of value is the basis of different types of business ecosystems and sustainable differentiation.

Let's look at an example.

The Half-Life of Capabilities—and the Imperative for a New 20 Percent

The Chamberlain Group makes garage door openers for both retail and commercial customers. They are by far the market leader, with over 60 percent of the retail market in the United States and a healthy competitive position in the commercial market. The average life span of their product is fifteen years, with a repeat purchase of the product running at well over 50 percent. Their growth is tied to the health of the home-building market: more homes built, more garage door openers sold. So, clearly, there are environmental conditions beyond their control. Having said this, they are in an enviable position financially—no surprise, given their hefty market share. Margins are high, growth is solid, and opportunities for expansion are clear.

But even here, competitive clouds exist. Businesses are optimized for conditions that gave rise to them. As conditions change, however, what they were optimized for loses its relevance. They find themselves within a Red Queen race. The same holds true with a company as seemingly impervious to her charms as Chamberlain. Because conditions change.

All assets have a half-life of competitive relevance. No surprise here. We know that products last only so long, as customer expectations change, markets shift, and technologies evolve.[13]

Chamberlain recognizes this, as do many product or durables companies. They also recognize the need to shift from selling products to selling services.

Other companies have already done this, as illustrated by Schneider

---

13   *Business Ecosystems Come of Age*, Deloitte University Press, 2015, accessed October 14, 2016, http://dupress.com/periodical/trends/business-trends-series/.

Electric's shift from characterizing themselves as a product company that sells air compressors to a services company that sells the usage and business outcomes of their compressors. Rather than merely selling air compressor units, Schneider Electric now also sells *access* to and *usage* of them. Clearly the way they engage with their customers has had to change, not only in terms of the contracts they use and prices they charge but also the types of people they identify as potential clients. These types of changes are a key consideration (and concern) for a number of companies as they explore new ways to engage with customers, stakeholders, and markets. They are wary, appropriately, of cannibalizing what worked before and not knowing what they need to work on going forward.

Chamberlain is no different. Environmental conditions are changing, shifting how they view their ongoing competitive relevance. Software and services will become their differentiators, and products their enablers, not their differentiators.

New major and global companies are beginning to influence different parts of what was once Chamberlain's purview, namely their distribution channels via direct access to consumers. A variety of other trends portend potential clouds on the horizon of ongoing growth, including—

- Cars and homes quickly becoming connected, threatening Chamberlain's traditional accessory and licensing business models

- Millennials being more likely to rent than purchase homes and use automated car services rather than purchase them, impacting the total number of potential new customers

Chamberlain's challenge stems from their success. They are dominant in their industry, making it difficult to stop doing what they are doing and how they are doing it. Yes, clouds have formed, but change is hard. Just ask Blockbuster.

Our cautionary note to Chamberlain, and every company, is that the core capabilities that made you successful up to now no longer will. You will need a new 20 percent of capabilities to drive explosive growth.

Figuring out what these are is aided by insight into the half-life of your existing (and potential new) capabilities. Why is this?

Because the world changes.

Chamberlain's retail product lasts for years and supports a high repurchase rate. Is this growth sustainable in the future? Not likely, without dramatic reconfiguration and insight into what it is that drives the value of the product.

> Businesses are optimized for conditions that gave rise to them. But as conditions change, what they were optimized for loses its relevance. They often find themselves running the Red Queen race. The implication? The imperative to identify the new 20 percent of capabilities to capture 70 percent of the new value. Spoiler alert. The 20 percent that made you successful yesterday will be different from the 20 percent that underpins your growth tomorrow.

Product life cycles are getting shorter. Given this, many companies focus on speeding up their innovation cycle, getting more products or sending services out the door faster. These products and services rest largely on a specific set of underlying core capabilities, assets, or competencies. The problem is, the half-life of these capabilities is decreasing and, like shifting sand, creates a relentless imperative to spin out more and more products or services to stay in the same place relative to others—which is why it is critical to identify what the new 20 percent of critical capabilities on which your products and services should be built need to be.

Recently we were working with the head of strategy and digital transformation at a national health insurance company in the US with offices globally. We were talking through the implications of market shifts and the new 20 percent critical to driving nonincremental, explosive growth. At one point, he had an "aha" moment where the puzzle pieces of new business models, their implications for engaging with customers, the role of cognitive and analytic insights, and the new 20 percent came together. He stood up, paced around the room, and said, "Our old 20 percent, our 'control point of value,' has always rested on our capabilities to price risk and underlying risk books we use to create our products.

"What happens," he continued, "as the market shifts and our core business changes from pricing risk to preventing accidents? A lot . . . with implications we are only now starting to understand but have not yet grappled with."[14]

This is a wonderfully clear articulation of the challenge—and opportunity—to clarify what the 20 percent of critical capabilities once were and will need to be.

Several years ago, Chamberlain went through an exercise to identify its core capabilities underlying what it delivered. They described "motors on a stick," or motors embedded inside garage door openers, as one of their three core assets crucial to supporting their product and market position. Distribution channels—the big-box stores, such as Lowe's and Sears—reflected their second asset. The third was their OEM installation network of typically small independent contractors who installed their product.

Each of these assets—motors, distribution channels, and independent contractors—has a different half-life of ongoing relevance. Each faces different types of pressure that will affect how long they provide sustainable advantage.

The unique motors they've created face pressure from increasing mobile and integrated devices that manage the use of products like Nest or Amazon's Alexa. Nest started out as a heat monitoring application, but its functionality has broadened to include a range of home needs, personalizing its performance based on the behaviors of its users. The application not only monitors how frequently you use each room in your house but also can adjust your temperature room by room based on your preferences and your usage. Even this basic connectivity capability from Nest puts pressure on (or highlights opportunities for) Chamberlain and other

---

14   Seattle Innovation Roundtable, January 2017.

similar companies with single-use products. Again, using Chamberlain as an example, though many others fall into this camp, those who rely on big-box stores for their distribution face pressure as consumers purchase more goods online. There is even pressure on the independent contractors who install Chamberlain's or other companies' stand-alone products. As large online companies like Amazon expand their services from home delivery to home installation, what happens to Chamberlain's existing support infrastructure, particularly if the new services are easier to use, more convenient, and cheaper?

These examples highlight a blunt reality: the decay rates of the assets that have made many companies successful to date may be accelerating. (Of course, it works the other way too. The core asset underlying your business may be accelerating in value as well—a topic we'll return to later.)

What does this mean for you? It means getting insight into (a) what your core assets are and (b) what your decay (or accelerating) rates are for each asset and what's driving them (differently, since each asset has a unique half-life).

Five Questions to Answer—Based on Thinking about Your Assets This Way

- **What are the few assets that drive the majority of your market value?**

  There tend to be no more than five to seven assets that support your value, regardless of the size of your company. For Chamberlain, it was their motor, distribution channel, and independent network of installers.

  What are yours?

- **What is the half-life of those assets?**

  Products and advantages only last so long, as customer expectations change, markets shift, and technologies evolve. ING, a global insurance group, went through this exercise and identified five key assets, one of which was their ability to identify and allocate risk. Risk identification requires gathering tremendous amounts of information about individuals—both demographic and behavioral data. When the explosion of easily obtainable data from social media and other public sources emerged in the past decade, ING estimated that the half-life of the risk information they identified as an asset had changed dramatically. The information they had reduced in relevance to eighteen months, down from thirty-six months just a few years earlier.

What is the half-life of your assets?

- **What is the directional rate of change of those assets?**

While some assets remain quite stable, others decay quite quickly (as did the relevance of a specific type of risk data to ING), and some increase in value (such as the recommendation engine that powers a significant amount of customer up-sell on Amazon). The rate of change (which can be depicted as a slope on a curve) determines the duration of value of that asset. The flatter the curve, the longer its relevance; the sharper, the shorter its relevance or the greater the importance of one asset over another.

What is the direction—and timing of ongoing relevance—of your key assets?

- **What impacts those rates of change?**

What environmental conditions or activities exist "out there" that impact what you are doing "in here," within your business?

Activities affect your assets and consequently their ongoing relevance. You have zero to minimal control over some of these activities, and some to significant control over others. The plunging commodity prices in 2015, or the overall lackluster GDP growth in China or the US, impacted many businesses in ways they had no capability to influence. On the flip side, changing distributors or supply networks from one part of the world to another is something that businesses can control.

What are the key activities that positively or negatively impact the ongoing relevance of your assets—those you can control and those you can't?

• **How do you change those rates, whether up or down?**

Changing these rates of competitive relevance requires investing time and resources. For Chamberlain, the role of big-box stores is to influence possible customers to purchase its garage door openers. Those stores' role in influencing customers is waning as their share of home purchasing gets challenged by new online competitors. Assuming Chamberlain wanted to protect the role of influencing customers through box store relationships, it would need to change the rate of relevance of this asset-requiring investment. Getting insight into such rates both helps clarify the competitive half-lives of key assets that drive the majority of your value and provides insight into what it would take to maintain, enhance, and/or reduce their ongoing relevance.

Which of those activities "out there" can you influence, and which offer you zero opportunity to do so? What can you do within your business, or ecosystem, to change that slope? Do you even want to?

Two Lessons from Chamberlain

The Chamberlain example highlights two key considerations underlying a new value framework from an ecosystem perspective.

First, there are key capabilities that underlie what it is you deliver—no matter your industry, your size, or your geography. Knowing what these are—and getting alignment around these—is challenging but critical to sense what's changing and to identify potential opportunities in order to take advantage of those changes.

Second, there is a decay rate (and the obverse, an acceleration rate) of key capabilities. Knowing what these are is equally challenging yet arguably even more critical to ensuring you can keep playing the competitive game.

The example so far focused on two pragmatic frameworks to help begin to answer the question, What capabilities do we need to build to capture new sources of value? However, you may have noticed that we haven't yet answered the logical preceding question: Where *do* we focus, and what are our new foundations of value? Let's return to an example introduced in Chapter 1 to answer this question.

New Foundations of Value—Because Markets Change

Market conditions, customer requirements, and technology affordances change, which means that the relevance of capabilities that have generated much of your value to date will change as well. The half-life of your assets is affected by the pace at which these conditions, requirements, and affordances change—which leads to one conclusion (out of your control) and one implication (completely in your control).

First, the conclusion: businesses tend to be optimized for a world that no longer exists—which is why insight into (a) what the half-life of your assets happens to be and (b) what it would take to change that half-life becomes of operational importance.

Second, the implication: identify where to play within the newly understood ecosystem, the new foundations of value. Knowing that will prioritize what your new 20 percent needs to be. To rephrase this, your new 20 percent makes up your capabilities critical to capturing your *new foundations of value*. Let's explain how.

Let's return to Dylan Garnett, the CEO of Metropolitan Health, for an example.

Metropolitan Health is Africa's largest health insurance third-party administrator, which we've discussed elsewhere to illustrate other points. As a reminder, South Africa is planning on nationalizing its health-care system to cover its approximately 52 million people, of which only 8 million had coverage as of 2016. The effect on every business that touches health care—both by SIC code and other businesses, such as telecommunications, financial services, and technology—is profound.

If you strip away all of the complexity of the considerations of key actions and actors, behaviors and policies, and delivery and payment models that underlie care delivery, you end up with what Dylan called the essential market, which needs to deliver "more care for more people." He went on to describe these needs as "the only requirements that matter regarding health-care transformation. They form the new foundation of value . . . all other activities and requirements being subsets of, or support of, meeting the essential market needs."[15] These market needs are listed below:

- **Increasing affordability.** A critical challenge facing Dylan—and frankly anyone who focuses on health system transformation—is how to get people who cannot afford health care to get it. Doing so is critical not only for reasons of societal equity but also economic sustainability of health-care delivery over time. The high costs of health-care delivery crowd out other public investments. It also limits benefit packages to employees, which serves to push out costs until later and impacts employee attraction and retention rates. High costs also impact broader labor and hence economic productivity over time if people become unable to get the care needed when they need it.

- **Enabling access.** Getting people to the right care provider for the right reason at the right time is a challenge globally. It is extremely difficult in areas with limited care professionals. Enabling access is critical for two key reasons. First, the divide between the haves and have-nots regarding health care in South Africa (and everywhere) needs to be bridged; this has become a critical requirement for the new health policy initiative.

  Second, greater access strengthens risk-profiling of the population and hence greater insight into effective care delivery. This in turn leads to greater predictive and preemptive interventions over time, as patterns of efficacy get determined by more and more cases being seen, treated, and reported.

  Again, this requirement is not unique to Africa. We broadened the definition of access with Dylan because of a specifically

---

15   Discussion, November 10, 2013, Cape Town.

challenging condition it faced: there are significantly fewer care professionals in South Africa per population than there are in other parts of the world, and this ratio gets much worse when you go out to the villages, many of which lack the types of infrastructure—water, roads, physical—that we take for granted elsewhere.[16]

What many have, however, even in the remotest of villages, is a cell phone. Perhaps not a smartphone, with lots of apps on it, but at least a text-based phone, more than serviceable for talking and messaging. So access, for us, was expanded to include access to mobile devices that could be used to communicate and engage those who needed care and those who could deliver it. This mattered for a simple reason. As discussed previously, different capabilities need to be delivered by different kinds of organizations and orchestrated by the point person in the ecosystem—in this case, CEO Dylan. Nontraditional partners critical to providing access, based on our expanded definition, included pharmaceutical companies (that provided the drugs), mobile carriers (that provided the mobile devices and services), and SAB (South African Brewery, that provided distribution and logistics support in delivering materials and mobile devices out to the villages), among others.

- **Driving outcomes.** There continues to be debate throughout the US, Europe, and much of the world in terms of how to measure effective health outcomes. The Affordable Care Act of 2010, the United States' significant transformation in terms of how health care is delivered and paid for, has taken significant strides in shifting payment mechanisms from payments for services rendered (which incentivized care professionals to perform more services, whether or not they were needed) to outcomes realized (which incentivizes care professionals to deliver the right type of care at the right time). Given this realization, outcomes matter because they help

---

16   For one quick comparison, South Africa has .76 physicians per 10,000 people compared with 2.42 per 10,000 in the United States. Index Mundi, accessed December 28, 2015, http://www.indexmundi.com/g/r.aspx?v=2226.

decrease costs and increase economic productivity (given that people get well faster and stay healthy longer), thereby reducing the overall economic burden of health-care costs, which allows other societal investments to be made.

In short, there are three essential foundations of value underlying any health system: affordability, access, and outcomes. What Dylan had to figure out was which set and how much of these foundations he wanted (and could) focus on. Figuring that out determined what his new 20 percent needed to be to deliver more care for more people.[17]

Many of these capabilities were new to Metropolitan Health. Many also were not ones that even made sense for Metropolitan Health to hold in-house. For example, enabling access required providing mobile devices to people throughout the country and the capturing of source—switch—data of usage, which was controlled by mobile carriers. The orchestration of these new capabilities, pulled from two very different types of businesses, required a new business process (of partnership engagement), technology capability (of switch-data analysis integrated with medical records), and design capability (of creating both visually simple or text-based care advice or recommendations)—all part of the new 20 percent critical to capturing the new sources of value that *more care for more people* required.

Two Lessons from Dylan Garnett

First, insight into where value is being created and destroyed within the ecosystem in which you and your customers are engaged will direct you toward the possible new foundations of value. The challenge is figuring out which of these you want and can "own."

Remember: business ecosystems are orchestrated around essential types of value to deliver. *Essential* is the key word. It reflects the abstraction of the key foundations—or essence—of value that underlie industry transformation around new customer needs. Despite the seemingly

---

17   Two-day workshop, November 22, 2013, Stellenbosch, South Africa.

chaotic complexity, the essential foundations of value underlying *any* health-care system are straightforward. They rest on affordability, access, and outcomes. Retail has its own essential foundations of value: convenience, speed, and radical simplicity. Other markets have similar essential foundations of value. *What are yours?*

Second, it is impossible for any one firm, or industry, to be masters of all of the foundations of value and the capabilities needed to be so— which is why the discipline of articulating what these foundations are becomes so important: to force a discussion around what foundations made you successful up to today and what will be critical for driving explosive growth tomorrow. Answering these questions requires knowing the specific market breakdown or customer need to focus on. But once you know this, you can distill the essential foundations of value that create new opportunities for growth and impact.

Yet even here, as in the case of Dylan, you have to make a choice in terms of what foundation of value you will focus on. No one has the resources or capabilities to be world-class at all of them at the same time. The relevance of this framework is to drive alignment around the new foundations of value for a specific market need. Its impact lies in forcing executives to choose which of these foundations to focus on—including when, where, and how.

There's another key consideration underlying this discussion of new foundations of value and the choice of which one(s) to focus on. A major one. An extremely difficult one. One that goes straight to the heart of who you are and what you do. Let's take a look.

Implication for Who You Are and What You Do, and Why Transformation Is So Hard: Wisdom from Winston

Winston Churchill, one of the UK's longest-serving and most important prime ministers, used to say that it was important to hear what politicians said but critical to watch what they did. Replace the word *politicians* with the *words business executives and the companies they oversee*, and a stark reality emerges. There is frequently a difference between what the executives say their business is—the Standard Industrial Classification (SIC) label attached to it—and what it really is and does.

What *is* Amazon, from an identity perspective? According to SIC codes, it is a commerce organization. And it is, from one perspective. But Amazon characterizes itself as a data analytics company (based on the company's recommendation and customer-insights engines), a cloud service provider (based on its hosting business, which until late 2015 was the only part of the company that had been profitable), certainly an e-commerce company, and potentially even more.

What is Uber, or BMW for that matter? Uber is a technology company to be sure, but it is also a transportation company, a data analytics company, and a health-care delivery company as it expands its capabilities to serve specific market needs. And BMW? It's clearly a luxury automobile company. Yet as the new marketplace of connected cars explodes in size due to new sets of capabilities—a new 20 percent of wireless connectivity and data services—BMW is exploring changing how it might price a car, from selling it as a product to subscribing to the services (of convenience and data) while you drive the car.

Why Winston Matters

Customers change, markets shift, and technologies evolve. This evolution changes what people expect and consequently where value is created and destroyed. With what imperative? The imperative of the new 20 percent— requiring that you rethink where and how to play. The effects on what you do and how you do it are profound. Equally profound is the implication for who you are—your identity and the *why* of what it is you do.

Moss Adams is a leading accounting and advisory firm on the West Coast of the United States, headquartered in Seattle. Like every accounting, tax, and consulting firm—irrespective of size and global footprint—Moss Adams faces similar challenges: how, in the world of machine learning and AI, do they continue to provide their fiduciary responsibilities to clients using their existing (to date) tried-and-true business practices and model?

Their core business model is people driven and based on hourly billing. The more people they have as clients, the higher their utilization rates and the more money they make.

Machine learning and other firms of analytic insights threaten (as well as create exciting new opportunities for) Moss Adams. A focused algorithm can churn through text, numbers, and models far faster and with far fewer errors and inconsistencies than an army of people from advisory firms. The need of their clients remains the same: transparent accountability. The value proposition also remains the same: trust and fiduciary responsibility. However, the mechanism of delivering that proposition in this industry is at the doorstep of a radical market shift.

For Moss Adams, KPMG, E&Y, and all of the other successful advisory firms, the answer is clear: double down on their fiduciary value proposition and reevaluate their existing business model of how they engage their clients and how they orchestrate their capabilities to do so. They have had to reconsider what has made them successful and what will have to change—not in terms of fiduciary responsibilities but certainly in how they deliver value to their clients. For one of these companies, a key was going back to the company's first principles. One of their COOs remarked that her company had to "reassess our core principles and identity of what we stood for" in a changing world.

Her insights are instructive. Rethinking what their *why* was—their mission or identity—helped her and her team recognize that how they delivered on their value proposition needed to change. The competitive lines that her industry lives in are blurring. This blurring created the opportunity for a bold leader like this particular COO to revisit what their core value proposition was and what their corresponding identity needed to reflect.

Identifying Your Core Assets—and Identity

Identity matters. It rallies people, articulates what you stand for, and provides a direction toward the type of impact you can have; consequently it guides the types of capabilities you'll need. An ecosystem perspective suggests how to reframe this identity in a shifting world.

Typically, organizations tie their identity to their SIC code—e.g., "We are <fill in the blank: a bank, a telco, a car company, a manufacturing company, an ecommerce company>." And consequently, "Our capabilities are mapped to the value chain that makes up what we are." Given this truth, it is not surprising that so many mission statements look and sound similar—e.g., "We intend to be the market-leading company delivering best-in-class products and services to our customers." These mission statements are completely internally focused, nondifferentiating, and begging to be disrupted by new entrants.

The following is a simple but pragmatic exercise we frequently use to help organizations review their first principles in order to help them rethink who they are, given new (potential) roles to play within an ecosystem.

Rather than sticking to the traditional "we are an X company," an ecosystem perspective suggests that you start with "the market needs we meet are Y, and consequently the essential value we offer to meet those needs are Z, and the essential capabilities—the 20 percent needed to do so—consist of A, B, and C." This approach has and, we believe, will always lead to a different set of what constitutes A, B, and C—the new 20 percent of critical capabilities tightly mapped between why you do what you do and the value proposition you offer your customers.

Cisco provides a clear example of a shifting identity and the implications that resulted. Cisco's identity shift over the past fifteen years has had material implications for how it engages its customers, its core assets, and consequently how it revitalized its growth.

Cisco recognized that building routers, while critical for driving consumer and business Internet-enabled connectivity, was commoditizing quickly. Cisco's leadership team recognized the need to focus on a new set of core assets critical to keeping them in the driver's seat in terms of how their customers and industries get and stay online. They shifted their strategy away from the manufacturing and distribution of routers to the design, architecture, and establishment of standards and protocols that enable connectivity of all kinds.[18] Using the framework we're suggesting, the decay rate of manufacturing and distribution of routers was accelerating quickly, whereas focus on the design and architecture of connectivity was identified as a new and rapidly accelerating source of more sustainable, longer-term value to capture.

One Lesson from the Identity Game

We have found the exercise "we are X and consequently the game is Y" to be as provocative as it is pragmatic. An ecosystem perspective helps teams make sense of their competitive landscape differently. It stress tests their assumptions about what has driven and what could drive value.

All businesses have *foundations of value*, as Metropolitan Health's Dylan Garnett calls them, upon which most of what they do rests. These foundations shift as technology innovations, customer expectations, and markets change. It's easy to forget this, particularly when we put more products and services out in the market without fundamentally reassessing the foundations of value all of them are based on. "Excavating back" to these foundations is hard, but critical. The "we are X and consequently the game is Y" exercise helps you dig to your foundations. It forces a focus on the essential assets that support what you do. The exercise creates a conversation around the previous, existing, and future foundations of value. It also begins to identify what these new foundations may be and when you need to start caring about them.

Three Considerations for a New Framework of Value (So Far)

Ecosystem-centric business models are built on a new framework of value. This chapter began to lay out key elements underlying that framework. The elements discussed so far begin to—

---

18   Bronwyn Fryer and Thomas Steward, "Cisco Sees the Future," *Harvard Business Review*, Nov. 2008, accessed Dec. 15, 2015, https://hbr.org/2008/11/cisco-sees-the-future.

- Provide a structured way to explore where to focus for explosive growth

    Stated differently, explosive growth will come from planting a flag around specific market challenges or customers you will "own," identifying the essential foundations of value that meet those needs, figuring out what the critical capabilities are (the new 20 percent) that underlie each of those foundations.

- Catalyze a discussion about where value is being created and destroyed within the ecosystem in which you are engaged and the core capabilities you need to take advantage of them

    These elements guide a reconsideration of what has been driving your value yesterday and today, and it explores what might deliver new sources of value tomorrow. *Spoiler alert: it will have little if anything to do with new products or services.* Banks seem to create new products and services weekly. Yet their underlying asset value doesn't come from these. Nor does Chamberlain's value come from its core retail product, even though as of 2016 it had a robust market share. Nor does Cisco's core asset value come from its multiple connectivity products. Core capabilities change as markets and customer needs change.

    The ongoing relevance of your critical capabilities is impacted by both actions you can and those you can't control. Insight into their half-life requires taking an ecosystem perspective. And, once you begin doing so, you are led logically to their reconsideration of what makes up your new 20 percent of assets—products, services, skill sets, technology, and processes—needed to capture the new sources of value.

    Another spoiler alert: *the new 20 percent will not be the same as the 20 percent that made you successful before.* Cisco recognized this, shifting the skill sets, partnerships, and how they engaged the market over the past fifteen years toward their new value in connectivity standards and architectural design. Chamberlain will work through the implications as it rethinks how to *bend* its asset curves around its core assets of distributors and agents.

What will you work through as you review your *why* and *what you do* in a changed competitive world?

- Encourage a reconsideration of who you are, what problems you want to "own" in the market, and consequently how you position yourself within the market as you decide which set of new foundations you want to focus on.

All good, for a start. But business ecosystems orchestrate capabilities from different partners in service of a common objective. How do you do that, given that different stakeholders care, or are motivated by, different types of value? That's what we'll explore in the next chapter, returning to Mark and his intent to create explosive growth through his big-bet portfolio.

3

Currencies and Getting
Different Folks to Play Together

You get, as the adage goes, what you measure. Since what you measure is what motivates behavior, hopefully that behavior is aimed at the value you want to realize. Value means different things to different people. Given this and to no surprise, you will get different behaviors aimed at realizing different types of value. So a question becomes, How do you mobilize behavior from different actors who care about different types of value in a common direction? That's a critical challenge regarding capturing new types of value from an ecosystem perspective. So what do you do? You take pragmatic steps. Let's see how.

The Criticality of Currencies

Different stakeholders within an ecosystem care about different types of value. Each of these different types of value *is* measurable. Let's call each of these different types of value a *currency*. A currency, then, is a different type of value that motivates the behavior of different stakeholders. That's the short definition. The slightly longer one is this: a currency reflects a different type of value that is meaningful (important to people), material (can be measured), and motivational (gets people to act in certain ways).

Why does this matter? Because ecosystems consist of different actors, many of whom are motivated by different types of value.

If motivation is driven by different types of value, then don't we need to have a common way to figure out (a) what *does* matter and (b) how to get more of it to those who care about it? That's where the concept of currencies comes in.

Currencies give people who care about different types of value a common language describing what matters to them in a way that makes each different type of value equal. No one type of value—dollars in the door, sustainability, patient outcomes, brand equity, etc.—is more or less important. This equivalency is critical when our business model is based on orchestrating different capabilities from different actors toward a common objective.

Back to Mark and How to Get Big Value Out of His Big-Bet Portfolio

Pragmatically, how does, and did, this exploration of value from an ecosystem perspective play out in Mark's company and its search for explosive growth as measured by net new revenues?

Regarding how to measure the value of a big-bet portfolio, it became clear that it isn't possible to separate discussions of value from the considerations about how to capture it. We had to break the initial question of "when will we be net cash positive?" into two questions, one a value measurement question and the second an execution one.

The first question was modified to "when will we realize different types of value under different (market and competitive) conditions? And what are the currency bundles—the different types of value—being created within the R&D and innovation portfolio?" The second question became "what can we do within our ecosystem to speed up and increase the amount of value we will create and share across different stakeholders?" The first questions were answered through simulations of different possible competitive scenarios, the last through data visualizations of new ecosystems that the innovation programs would impact.[19]

---

19 Scenarios are not intended to be either right or wrong. Rather, they aim to build a shareable language around what might be possible. Perspectives on what might be possible clarifies what activities or capabilities might be needed either to influence or respond to one or more of the scenarios.

Simulations were run to answer a specific question: When are we likely to realize value under different conditions? Different simulations explored a range of possible outcomes based on whether or not different activities come to pass. The degree of local manufacturing, energy costs, regulatory shifts, and the maturation of specific technologies were the major levers or sets of activities underlying this particular set of scenarios. Change any of these by moving the levers, having them more or less likely to happen, and the likelihood of any particular future, or scenario, changes.

Key to making the simulations relevant was the design and use of a currency map. A currency map clarified different types of value that different stakeholders cared about, including carbon footprint, income streams, and brand equity. As scenarios played out, the types of value that resulted in differing amounts shifted accordingly. Tangible implications came, and come, out of this way of thinking.

I. Currencies Help Create a Common Language

Currencies help create a common language to make sense of and wrestle through questions around how to prioritize investments based on different criteria, or types of value, that matter to an organization.

Surely you've been in meetings where folks used the same words and appeared to be in agreement, but when they went back to their office, they commented, "I know what we said, but I'm not sure what we agreed to." People may have used the same words but meant different things, leading to misalignment. The very exercise of creating possible worlds or scenarios typically forces people to think about possibilities in new ways and thereby reduce the semantic disconnect that so often exists among different stakeholders. One output of this exercise is the creation of a new shared language about what might be possible and what types of value might be created around which to drive alignment.

What does having a common language do? To answer this question, let's go back to our example.

Those who care about carbon emissions often struggle to communicate the value of reducing one's carbon footprint to others who care about bringing net new cash in the door. The former is squishy; it's hard to assess when lower emissions will impact you, and it's impossible as an organization to predict (much less control) their material impact on the business. The value of new cash flow is the opposite; it is directly measurable, has clear timing implications, and you (for the most part) can directly influence it. Given that, it's no surprise that much discussion on carbon emissions falls into the category of CSR (corporate social responsibility) or PR (public relations) rather than core business areas. A challenge with many CSR initiatives and definitions of value is that they are easily dismissed, a "nice-to-have" but expendable when budgets are tight. Yet there are powerful changes afoot in sustainability as a currency, even prior to the Paris 2015 Climate Agreement Framework, which will play out for decades to come.

A common language across stakeholders in terms of what they care about injects rigor into the decision-making process. No longer will decisions be (solely) based on those who yell the loudest. Currencies, as an equivalency unit of value, bridge the semantic gaps that so often exist among different folks.

2. A Common Language Makes It Easier to Clarify Trade-Offs

Let's extend the example around sustainability to explain how a common unit of value is useful to clarify trade-offs.

Europe has been at the forefront of figuring out how to create what is known as an *equivalency* of value for carbon emissions. They have been doing so through modifying the SASB (Sustainability Accounting Standards Board) accounting standards for sustainability. SASB, as of 2016, recognized that the translation of environmental, social, and other so-called externalities (a side-effect or consequence that impacts other parties within it being captured in the cost of its creation) cannot be clearly equated with many financial measures. However, SASB has a reasonable argument that the rigorous FASB (Financial Accounting Standards Board) definition of materiality provides a bridge to a more rigorous grounding that allows comparisons across different types of value.

The two concepts that are newly linked are *socially shared capital* (externalities) and *materiality*. These two elements, arguably, could sway institutional investor portfolio decision making and impel a far more pragmatic step toward building a common language than the current "finger in the air impact rating."[20] In other words, if you mess up the water supply in township X, you're undermining my investment of real estate in that same township. This is different from the internal or issuer accounting, traditionally centered on revenue or cost. *SASB seeks to impose the same legal standard of materiality for companies to report on externalities from an investor portfolio point of view.*[21] Historically, that "reasonable investor" may not have had the fiduciary responsibility for ethical investments for its portfolio. Now it seems that the disclosure of externalities is part of whatever the portfolio mandate is. This could be a game changer.[22]

Here's an example of how this has played out for a particular business. Executives can, and do, use currencies to have frank conversations about the common trade-offs across different types of value they might want to capture. Currencies provide an equivalency language for doing so. One company we worked with recognized that the carbon emissions game in Europe was moving far faster than in the US. The executives came to the conclusion that whatever came out of SASB would find its way, in some form, into US accounting—or GAAP—standards at some point in the future. Consequently, getting ahead of the curve in terms of carbon-based accounting in ways similar to how SASB defined and accounted for this type of value could become a market differentiator.

---

20   Sustainability Accounting Standards Board website, accessed January 10, 2017, https://www.sasb.org.

21   The definition states: "SASB follows the definition of materiality adopted by US Securities laws and case law. Information is material if there is 'a substantial likelihood that the disclosure of the omitted fact would have been viewed by the reasonable investor as having significantly altered the "total mix" of information made available.'"

22   Additionally, SASB standards provide disclosure guidance and accounting standards for a minimum set of sustainability issues or topics that have a significant material impact on most, if not all, companies in an industry. Immense thanks to Jeff Pappin, a great friend, for this insight.

This insight led them to reprioritize the timing and resources committed to their projects based on carbon footprint, even though the financial return on these projects was neither clear nor immediate.

Currencies provided them a common language for defining value and motivating different types of actors. This was particularly important because their "big bet" was based on working with a number of different types of firms, many with different capabilities and motivations. It became a useful new way to help them answer the question, "When will we realize different types of value under different conditions?"

3. Currencies Help Prioritize What Capabilities Are Needed and When

Exploring possibilities leads to discussions of what capabilities are needed to capture different types of value, as well as how and when to do so. The business logic of the twentieth century and that of the past decade has been to grow big, build competitive moats, control your supply chains, and play the zero-sum game, namely, "I win, you lose." The logic of today's explosive growth and that of tomorrow is different. It is about creating new sources of value in new ways through orchestrating assets and skill sets across different partners that all play the positive-sum game, namely, "If we win, we all win."

Businesses are optimized for a world that no longer exists. What made them successful yesterday is absolutely not what will make them effective tomorrow.

Most people recognize this, but as markets, regulations, expectations, and technologies change, so too do the capabilities needed to succeed and the methods to orchestrate them. This, of course, is why innovation has become so critical and why so much attention is paid to being agile and able to adapt with speed and scale to whatever the future will bring.

The blunt reality is that tomorrow's competitive landscape requires a new business model, one that orchestrates capabilities from different firms. *Rarely will any particular firm have all of the capabilities needed to capture new sources of value.* Therefore, leaders will be faced with two critical questions:

- What capabilities will be needed to capture emerging sources of value?
- What will be our new 20 percent of critical capabilities to do so?

Clearly, we can't have all the capabilities (unless, of course, you are in the ranks of Google, Apple, Amazon, Tencent, and Facebook). So which ones do you focus on, which do you partner for, which do you monitor, and which do you ignore? And underlying these considerations is the key question: How *do* you orchestrate your ecosystem and the capabilities distributed throughout it so you capture the types and amounts of value that matter to you?

The revised question of "how do we capture different types of values under different conditions?" opens a rich, profound set of considerations. The concept of currencies is an important ingredient to add to your transformational stew.

But we're still missing another key ingredient. It's one thing to know what different types of value motivate behavior; it's another to know how that insight creates shareable value—that everyone gets more out of what they need. Doing so requires—no surprise—a new method of engagement, a new business model. Let's see how this has, and can, work.

The Rise of Shared Value as a Distinctive Competitive Strategy

Dean faced a challenge. Dean was corporate head of product development at one of the world's largest telecommunications companies headquartered in Europe. Global data traffic was expected to be more than ten times larger in 2017 than in 2012. This may sound like a good challenge from the telecommunication company's perspective, but it wasn't. Rapid growth comes from data usage, and many companies are focused

on delivering and capturing value from that usage. However, the firms
that tend to be capturing a lion's share of that value are not telcos but
are what are known as over-the-top (OTT) or other data firms, such as
WhatsApp, Weibo, and other messaging platforms that ride on top of
carrier networks.

Dean's challenge can be distilled into what is referred to within
the telecommunications industry as a *jaws chart*. This depicts the gap
between two different types of revenue over time: that accruing to voice
and that to data, with the former losing out to the latter in relevance and
quanta. The challenge stems from two sources:

- Data usage is driven by data providers. They capture a relatively larger share of the data revenue than do those providing
  the networks.

- While overall revenue for telcos has been increasing, the revenue
  contribution of voice traffic, the traditional money machine for
  telcos, has been declining relative to the contribution of data.

The question Dean had to answer, as does nearly every traditional
carrier on the planet, is how to close the gap depicted in a jaws chart in
an environment where the greater value (data) is captured by other players (the OTT guys).

Clearly, the OTT players and the traditional carriers needed each
other: one to provide the carrier backbone and the other to keep its pipes
filled with products of use to the customer. From the carrier perspective,
the OTT players were the ones who interacted with customers: they were
the ones who provided the mobile wallets, the instant messaging services,
the online games, and the apps. Consequently, the customers tended to
care more about the guys who provided them the services they wanted
than the carriers on whose networks they interacted. When Candy Crush
goes down, who are you going to call? Candy Crush or AT&T? The telcos well recognized that they were (and are) losing a critical relationship

with their customers, at least with respect to the big area of data applications and services. Getting these relationships back and closing the jaws chart are key explanations for why so many telcos around the world are creating what they call enterprise solutions—data-rich applications that customers care about and are demonstrably willing to pay for.

The question facing Dean and so many others is, How do you close the jaws chart in a way that benefits the different types of firms that have capabilities necessary to capture the new sources of value that customers care about? How do you align behavior from different organizations that have different incentives in a way that generates value for both? This was the opportunity that MoDe saw and took advantage of, as described earlier.

MoDe clearly articulated a market need, identified critical capabilities needed to meet it, recognized that these capabilities came from different types of firms (OTT, banking providers, and telcos), and orchestrated an ecosystem that increased the value to all of them while meeting that market need. Oh . . . and it closed the gap between the revenue coming from voice and that from data.

Ecosystems reflect the orchestration of different capabilities from a diverse set of actors. They require, and rest on, collective action toward the capturing of new, shareable value. No one can go it alone. First, no one has all the capabilities needed to do so. Second, much more value can be realized by mobilizing the very best capabilities different organizations have. Dean's answer has been to codesign a series of enterprise solutions that take advantage of the existing core capabilities of telcos (e.g., their physical networks) and to partner with other firms that bring new capabilities relevant to their corporate customers (e.g., cyber-threat risk insight and health-care content distribution). Their impact so far? We'll see. But the very process of getting different types of stakeholders in the room together and coming up with co-branded offerings toward tackling specific market friction that each of the firms cares about has been a solid start and extension to their traditional way of doing business.

Shareable Value and Wicked Problems

Getting business ecosystems to work rests on everyone getting more of what it is they need. That is clearly the only way to motivate collective and sustainable action across different types of organizations. How to do this pragmatically is what ecosystem models excel at. At the core of these models is the concept of shared value, whereby everyone engaged shares risk and return (however defined) and the premise that they will get more value from being part of an ecosystem than if they went alone.

Another way to illustrate the impact of business ecosystems and the pragmatics of how shareable value works is to provide a couple of examples of what traditionally have been impossible (or extraordinarily difficult—wicked) problems to tackle. Several characteristics make up *wicked problems*:

- They are so complex in terms of lots of moving parts, moving so quickly that no one organization can solve them on its own.

- They involve different types of stakeholders who are frequently motivated by different objectives and types of value, making it hard to align around.

- The economics underlying them don't work for any one organization. The risks far outweigh any economic reward for any single commercial business to take on.

A demonstrably effective way to solve wicked problems is to rely on new business models and methods of engagement. Business ecosystems are that new method of engagement. They help to shift the risk/reward balance, thereby changing the business and political logic of these difficult challenges. Key to holding together these business ecosystems is, as we will see in the two examples below, a shared value framework that respects and allocates different types of value to different types of actors in a way that everyone is incentivized to participate and help each other. Let's see how this has worked.

Example #1: Tackling Antimicrobial Resistance:
Coming Back from the Brink?

Antimicrobial resistance (AMR) is a growing and extraordinarily dangerous health crisis as declared by governments, professional societies, and the media. Infections caused by drug-resistant bacteria claim tens of thousands of lives in the developed world (and an estimated 500,000 worldwide) and cost billions of dollars each year.[23] Overuse of existing antibiotics and industry disinvestment in the development of new ones has led to ever-thinner lines of defense against emerging superbugs. Moreover, the absence of effective, rapid point-of-care diagnostics relegates doctors to rely on informed guesswork about what medicines a patient's infection might respond to in a situation where a few hours of delay in beginning an effective treatment can mean the difference between life and death.

The gap between the significant need for innovation in this arena and the meager returns to those who invest in it is a market failure. How so? The typical revenue model of pharmaceutical companies is based on setting as high a price as possible (to recoup investments in the drug discovery process) and selling as much as possible (for both the original intent of the drug and what's known as off-label uses—treating other symptoms that have been identified to which the drug can be applied). For the majority of pharmaceutical companies, investments are allocated in those areas where the simple price-times-sales model is projected to be the largest.

However, AMR does not follow this model. The more drugs used, the greater the resistance to the efficacy of those drugs. The less the effectiveness, the fewer the drugs sold, which causes the typical pharma model to break down. This explains why so few pharmaceutical companies invest

---

23   Kevin Outterson, John Powers, Gregory Daniel, and Mark McClellan, "Repairing the Broken Market for Antibiotic Innovation," *Health Affairs* 34, no. 2 (2015), accessed January 22, 2016, http://drive-ab.eu/wp-content/uploads/2014/09/Health-Aff-2015-Outterson-277-85.pdf. Also, "Toward a New Global Business Model for Antibiotics: Delinking Revenues from Sales," Chatham House Report, October 2015, and "New Business Models for Sustainable Antibiotics," Chatham House Centre on Global Health Security Working Group Papers (London, February 2014).

in this critical health area. The gap between the significant need for innovation in this arena and the meager returns to those who invest in this innovation has put the world population's health in a dire situation.[24] How to overcome this?

Clearly, doing so requires different types of organizations: private sector, public agencies, patients, caregivers, etc. This is a classic example where a public good—more effective antibiotics—requires both public and private sector innovation (to quote the social entrepreneur George Goldsmith). How do you align these very different types of actors in a way that motivates each of them and delivers value to all of them, despite the obviously different ways they are motivated and measure value?

Answering these questions requires an understanding of the different activities that make up the AMR ecosystem. Such insight begins to shed light into the various factors that interact with each other in a way that, to date, has stymied any productive move to tackle the wicked problem that is AMR.

The AMR ecosystem is made up of multiple (different types of) actors in complex interactions, with ripple effects highlighting the impossibility of tackling AMR in a piecemeal fashion. Many of these individual activities affect each other and are impacted by multiple organizations. You can carefully monitor what drugs get delivered to what patients, increasing the likelihood that the right patients get the right drug at the right time, but doing so reduces the incentive of the pharmaceutical companies. You could incentivize the pharmaceutical companies to make more drugs, but creating more drugs catalyzes a process to ensure that they are sold and used, leading to the problem we started out with—namely, overconsumption. This is a complex challenge with lots of interacting puzzle pieces, each controlled by different types of actors, all with bewildering ripple effects on each other. The result? An exacerbated gap between rising resistance and lagging innovation that results in more infections that cannot be treated effectively,[25] with—

24   Ibid.
25   Discussion with Kevin Outterson, July 2014.

- Increased mortality, morbidity, and health-care costs resulting directly from multiresistant infections—conservatively assessed at an annual cost to the US health care system between $21 and $34 billion[26]

- A decreasing viability of many modern medical procedures that control the likelihood and severity of associated infections

- An increased vulnerability to untreatable pandemic infections

The challenge is stark, yet the benefits of overcoming it are great. Economically, the market failure in rewarding antibiotics and diagnostics innovation is proof positive that society is misallocating resources. The economic costs of this misallocation are both certain (numbers of unnecessary deaths and high costs of care, including longer hospital stays and readmissions) and contingent (eroding value of modern medical procedures, and the risk of pandemic infections).

This is a crisis.[27]

Tackling AMR through Business Ecosystems

AMR is complex—with enormous numbers of moving parts, lots of different types of organizations motivated by different types of value, and the impossibility of any one organization being able to tackle the problem alone—which is why a number of them are finally coming together to do something about it, beyond talking.

As stated before, no one type of organization can solve this problem: health care surveillance organizations can report on the extent of the problem; health-care providers can report on the efficacy of treatment; pharmaceutical companies can invest in more effective medicines; and governmental agencies can provide funding beyond research to taking pragmatic action. But it requires insight into what motivates these

---

26 Jirka Taylor et al., *Estimating the Economic Costs of Antimicrobial Resistance: Model and Results* (Washington, DC, Rand Corporation, 2014): 2.

27 WBUR, "A Wake-Up Call on Antibiotic Resistance," May 2014, http://www.wbur.org/onpoint/2014/05/05/antibiotic-resistance-superbugs-who-cdc/.

different organizations and getting them to align around different parts of this extremely difficult problem to tackle it in an orchestrated manner; this requires new business models. Pharmaceutical companies are starting to reenter the market with their investment risks offset by government funding; clinicians are getting insight into the clinical treatments that work, critically from those that do not involve prescribing antibiotics; health associations and networks are designing more effective stewardship programs and providing more effective training at the point of care; and so on. The point? We wouldn't have gotten past merely talking about all this if we hadn't sought out pragmatic insights into what different stakeholders cared about. Nor would we have moved forward without new methods of engagement.

Let's look at another example also drawn from health care: a similar challenge, further steps taken, and similar lessons.

Example 2: Beyond the Pill—Where to Have What Type of Impact

Sir Andrew Witty, CEO of GSK, one of the world's largest pharmaceutical companies, once said, "You can remain in the drug business. But you can't remain in the drug business you've always been in."[28] It was imperative, he argued, for pharmaceutical companies to go "beyond the pill." The phrase "beyond the pill" suggests that there exists a complement to strengthen care delivery if pharmaceutical companies spent time on services to *wrap* as well as merely to *sell* their pills. This has been an increasingly accepted call to action, followed up by material action and investments. Johnson & Johnson has spent well over $500 million on innovation centers focused on health-adjacent solutions that complement their drug business. Merck has a $1 billion investment fund focused on finding health solutions and analytic services distinct from their drug business.[29]

---

28 Global Pharmaceutical, "Progressions: Navigating the Payer Landscape," 2014, http://www.ey.com/Publication/vwLUAssets/EY_Progressions_2014/$FILE/EY-progressions-2014.pdf.

29 Global Health Innovation Fund, "Leadership in Digital Health Investing," 2016, accessed Jan. 22, 2016, http://www.merck.com/ghi/.

What's going on?

We are seeing a range of experiments around how to engage customers differently. These experiments require capabilities from non-pharmaceutical companies—or at least something beyond the traditional ways pharmaceutical companies have approached their customers or their markets. Each requires orchestrating new capabilities from other organizations to do so. There are three points to highlight about these differing models.

First, they reflect different strategies to meet three key objectives that pharmaceutical executives all share: more engagement with patients, greater impact, and a restoring of patient trust. Other strategies rest on various business focuses, relationships, and sources of differentiation: people, process, actionable insight, and technology.

Second, each model requires distinctive partnership strategies as different types of firms enter the market. Urgent challenges to improve performance as measured by outcomes and cost have historically brought in new players with different ways of engaging with the market and customers. The business literature is littered with case studies of disruptive innovators that displaced seemingly entrenched and successful businesses. Health care is no different. Why else would Qualcomm and IBM, Apple and Samsung, Philips and Microsoft, Google and Amazon, Vodafone and British Telecom be investing billions of dollars into health care if not to take advantage of the changing rules of the game?

Third, these differing models each highlight a significant shift from focusing on cost controls to influencing stakeholders' behaviors in the hopes of realizing greater outcomes. The implications of this shift are profound and its questions challenging. Who does what? How does it get done? How are risks and rewards shared across a very different landscape of stakeholders? What new capabilities and assets are needed? How do we transition or ring-fence these new capabilities from what we already do? How do we lay the foundations for sustained impact? How do we motivate behavioral change? And critically, how do we make sure we don't cannibalize critical sources of existing profitability and revenue growth?

This is where and why wrap and beyond-the-pill strategies become compelling, and working through their operational implications challenging. They will become a critical strategy for transforming care management and strengthening trust across stakeholders to drive better patient outcomes. At the core of all of these rests the design and executional reliance of a shared value framework.

Ecosystems in Action: Two More Examples

A global pharmaceutical company is partnering with a telecommunications company, a medical device manufacturer, a global IT provider, a national payer, and several provider networks to provide an ecosystem-centric model to tackle diabetes in sub-Saharan Africa. Phase one focuses on rural villages, while phase two includes a rollout to metropolitan areas. This partnership has been designed around increasing awareness about diabetes and its implications, as well as increasing access to data that can provide insight into who has the condition and what to do about it. The collaborative effort is also developing targeted health-care and educational interventions based on different methods of social and technological engagement, whether mobile, social networks, or social media.

In another example, several pharmaceutical companies are moving aggressively to counter AMR. They are developing stewardship programs and calling for new return models (called *de-linkage* from de-linking revenue from the number of pills purchased). Ensuring that new and valuable antibiotics are only provided to patients who are known to be able to respond to them effectively is vital to making these programs work. In this example, the pharmaceutical companies are paid to not sell their pills. They are saved and used judiciously to minimize the risk of rampant resistance under a collaborative stewardship program made up of different stakeholders who design and monitor these programs and their effectiveness.

Both examples reflect business-model innovation, powered by ecosystem-centric strategies. The first one focuses on "owning" a therapeutic area, while the second seeks to perform the role of conductor for different players. They both require the orchestration of complementary products, services, and capabilities—ranging from analytics to process, improving adherence, and achieving both greater economic value and health outcomes.

Many other examples from around the world could be sketched. The intent, however, is less to enumerate examples than to suggest common implications of executing through shared value frameworks.

Two (More) Considerations Underlying a New Framework of Value

This chapter explored additional elements underlying a new framework of value, with two major implications.

- Currencies are a pragmatic mechanism to motivate behavioral change across folks who care about different types of value.

  As an *equivalency* unit of value, they put rigor into a decision-making process, making it less likely that decisions made will be based on the loudest voice in the room. They also help to formalize trade-offs between types of value, which is helpful in rethinking priorities of where to focus, when to do so, and with what type of expectations of impact.

- Shared value frameworks serve to monitor and adjust different types of stakeholder engagement against different types of value.

  The clarity of what motivates different stakeholders (via currencies) feeds into an execution framework to clarify what role each plays and the (new 20 percent of critical) capabilities they bring to the table—to help ensure that everyone is getting more of what they need.

  Bluntly, an ecosystem-centric business model will not work without insight into different types of currencies that motivate different types of behavior and an execution framework to monitor and adjust them.

In Closing—Learning from Wicked Problems

Health-system transformation, climate talks, implications of machine learning, ethical considerations in health technologies, investments in renewable energy systems, digital transformation, and cyber resilience are all examples of different types of wicked problems. Each is clearly too large for any one organization to address, involves many different types of organizations, and has an extraordinary number of interdependent activities to orchestrate. The only way to have any hope of tackling them effectively is to figure out how to motivate behavioral change from different types of organizations that care about different types of value.

Enter business ecosystems, an organizational model designed to align collective action toward shareable value. The crux of collective action from different types of actors rests on a shared value framework. Such a framework acknowledges, identifies, and clarifies that currencies, different types of value that motivate the behavior of different types of actors, exist. It serves to focus and monitor mechanisms of collaborative engagement so that value can be realized, orchestrated, and shared among the various parties.

This leads us to a final consideration regarding what makes up and how to capture value from an ecosystem perspective—namely, figuring out how to measure the total ecosystem opportunity (TEO), or potential value to be realized, and, arguably most importantly, which part of that TEO to focus on.

4

Total Ecosystem Opportunity (TEO)— or, What's in a Name?

Marc Andreessen and Jim Barksdale are good friends, stemming from their days when Marc designed Netscape, the Internet's first browser, and Jim funded and ran the Netscape Corporation. They have been extraordinarily successful at identifying and capitalizing on new sources of value, helping to catalyze the platforms of Internet-enabled business. When a new opportunity arises, they have a tag-team discussion on how to characterize where and how business value is created and destroyed given that opportunity.

They suggest that there are only two types of businesses: those that bundle and those that unbundle products or services. Business cycles tend to reflect trends in such bundling and unbundling as different phases seek to capture value that the preceding ones tend to trigger.[30] Amazon, Alibaba, and even Facebook are examples of firms that aggregate, or bundle, not only products and services but also different parts of their respective value chains. Extraordinary value is created for these firms as a result of the transaction efficiencies they realize. Today, many businesses and organizations

---

30 "Marc Andreessen and Jim Barksdale on How to Make Money," HBR IdeaCast, *The Harvard Business Review* (2014), accessed December 29, 2015, https://hbr.org/2014/07/marc-andreessen-and-jim-barksdale-on-how -to-make-money/.

seek to become platform-based to create the type of stickiness and new sources of value that these companies have demonstrated can be created.

Measuring TEO to Direct Your Focus

In Chapter 1 we described how explosive growth opportunities tend to be convergence plays where capabilities from different industries combine to meet a specific market or customer need. Safaricom's extraordinarily rapid growth in mobile money is an example of a convergence play. Convergence plays require taking an ecosystem perspective. Finding the new value in a business ecosystem requires insight into what we call the total economic opportunity (TEO) of your ecosystem. TEO is analogous to the concept of TCO (total cost of ownership). Over the years, TCO has become useful because it has helped many decision makers become aware of the direct and indirect, the observable and too often invisible, costs underlying technology investment decisions. Insight into one's TCO has led to more productive investments and focus. TEO does the same through providing insight into—

- Economic opportunities within a specific set of customer needs, some perhaps previously unseen and not captured

- Possible winners and losers as value shifts and the shape of ecosystems change

- Indications about where to focus effort to capture value quickly and at scale

Why Does TEO Matter?

- Like TCO, economic opportunities and costs are typically understated because we tend to measure what we see from industry perspectives. *Explosive value comes from the collision, overlap, or convergence across capabilities drawn from different industries, requiring new methods to identify both what these are and how to measure them.*

- Explosive values traditionally come from tackling friction or non-consumption, again requiring cross-capability methods both to identify and measure them.

- TEO frameworks help *make visible what is typically invisible* in terms of the actors across industries and the capabilities they bring to the table, as well as the specific sources of friction or breakdown they tackle.

Deloitte has estimated the TEO of the connected automotive industry.[31] Corwin, the lead author, estimates that the auto industry in the United States generated $2 trillion of annual revenue in 2014, 11.5 percent of US GDP. This included auto manufacturers, suppliers, dealers, financial services companies, oil companies, fuel retailers, aftermarket services and parts, insurance, public and private parking, public-sector taxes, tolling and traffic enforcement, medical care, and others. Converging forces are fundamentally shifting the future evolution of automotive transportation and mobility. They include, as Deloitte describes—

- Maturing technologies, such as battery and fuel-cell electric vehicles, that offer higher energy efficiency and lower emissions

- Innovative materials and technology, such as stronger and lighter materials that reduce vehicle weight without sacrificing passenger safety or the emergence of self-driving vehicles

- Rapid advances in connected vehicles via new vehicles being outfitted with vehicle-to-infrastructure, vehicle-to-vehicle, and communications technologies

- Shifts in consumer preferences as younger generations lean toward pay-per-use mobility instead of owning a car, or the Gen Y consumers using smartphone apps to plan travel so they can multitask as they do so.[32]

31 Scott Corwin et al., *The Future of Mobility: How Transportation Technology and Social Trends Are Creating a New Business Ecosystem* (New York: Deloitte University Press, 2015).
32 Ibid.

Corwin assessed the potential value shifts within the connected car ecosystem. Clearly we cannot know how these shifts will play out. A variety of different possible futures exist regarding when, how, and where the ecosystem will come to pass. These scenarios boil down to a per-mile summary cost calculation for different possible futures—ranging from $0.97 from incremental change to $0.31 for a new age of accessibility autonomy, with other options in between. What we do know, however, is that the future will reflect changes in the slope of the asset value of the core capabilities supporting today's automotive industry. The half-life of these assets will be impacted by—

- Regulation and government—including taxation and revenue, as well as laws governing capture, usage, storage, and the transfer of data

- Social attitudes—including perceptions about the role of human and machine interface, longstanding notions around vehicle ownership and usage, and continued growth of the sharing economy

- Technology development—including the acceleration of innovation or technology breakthroughs

- Privacy and security—including cyber-security and communication standards and protocols, as well as the protection of personal identification information

- Wall Street—including corporate valuations and investment capital availability

- Impacts to key stakeholders—including potential changes to current employment models, such as dislocation effects, costs, and change management[33]

Two trillion dollars, the TEO of the connected car industry, is far too big a number for any business to wrap its head around. Whether the

---

33   For a series of reports on these impacts, see Penn and Wihbey, "Uber, Airbnb and Consequences of the Sharing Economy." See also "Foundations and Current Issues in IR/HR (IRE 2001), University of Toronto Libraries, http://guides.library.utoronto.ca/c.php?g=251401&p=2686879, accessed February 12, 2017.

number is $2 or $2 trillion, however, the point is the same: *Insight into your TEO is a pragmatic exercise to clarify the new boundaries of what makes up your ecosystem.* A TEO also helps you focus on where different types of value are getting allocated to the actors who make up your ecosystem.

The Pragmatics of Ecosystem Economics: An Example from the Mobile Industry

The mobile industry has changed dramatically over the past ten years. If you compare those within this industry who provide connectivity—the carriers like AT&T, Sprint, Verizon, Orange, T-Mobile—with those who provide content and drive distribution—Google, Apple, Facebook, Amazon—you will see an astonishing difference. The market cap of just these last four companies exceeds all mobile carrier market cap globally by 30 percent. This is an astonishing turnaround for the former set of companies that have provided the dial tone of communications for decades.

Not surprisingly, Facebook declared a number of years ago that one of their objectives was to become the dial tone for the Internet. They, and other companies that drive wireless connectivity, have accomplished this. By doing so, they have catalyzed enormous shifts in value creation and destruction within the mobile ecosystem—yet in a way that is not a zero-sum game. The industry has transformed, blurring across industry lines. (Is there even such a thing as a phone or mobile carrier anymore?)[34] However, the mobile ecosystem, while shifting the distribution of value across different types of players, has certainly created new sources of value for those who figure out where and how to engage within it. These people recognize that their business model—again, merely a fancy word to represent how organizations organize and allocate their resources and activities—has changed.

As MobileVision aptly points out, the fundamental basis of competition in the mobile industry has shifted from the *reliability and scale of*

---

34 If so, what is the SIC code of that new player, given the blurring of industries engaged in this new domain called *mobility*?

networks to *choice and flexibility of services.*[35] They characterize this shift as the transition from mobile telephoning to mobile computing. This shift reflects the entrance of new players into a once well-defined industry as well as the evolution of new practices that have forever changed the game that the industry is playing.

The telecommunications industry grew around a tightly integrated set of core services: voice, SMS, and data access. It became vertically integrated (whereby they owned—or internalized—all of their value chain activities and assets) to provide these series with what are known as the *five nines* of reliability—referring to 99.999 percent uptime for access and use. Vertical integration was, at the time, critical for internalizing the risks of downtime and service outage.

As technology changed, the basis of competitive advantage changed to the choice and flexibility of services delivered. The relevance of vertical integration went down quickly and dramatically. Telcos could not respond fast enough to the range of services that customers demanded. They had neither the new 20 percent of critical capabilities nor the sufficient sensitivity to how customers wanted to use services. The implication? The share of needs and attention, as well as where folks were spending money, how service was being distributed, what counted as differentiation, and consequently the basis of competition, all changed as the industry moved from mobile telephony to the domain of mobile computing.

Mobile computing has changed the strategic game because it makes new types of organizations relevant. These new players have been enabled by smartphone platforms and application developers. They provide an extraordinarily rich set of options for services that customers initially wanted and then craved, shifting ever more demand away from the traditional carriers. Undifferentiated voice, text, and data—the workhorses of the old-school telco firms—started to run the Red Queen race. Value was clearly shifting to the new players. It appeared as though the market demand for so-called telco and wireless services provisioning was declining.

---

35   Vision Mobile, https://www.visionmobile.com.

Except, it was the opposite. The spend in the communication and wireless market grew and continues to grow exponentially. What needed to change was not the seeking of new sources of value but the business model used to capture them, in the sense that a rising tide of value was helpful for everyone—both traditional telco and OTT players. Dean, the telecommunications executive we referred to earlier, argued that viewing the OTT players as the new firms to compete against was to miss a great opportunity. For Dean, gaining insight into where value was being created and destroyed within the ecosystems in which he and his customers were engaged required a shift from a zero-sum, "us-versus-them" mentality to a collaborative approach.

> The blunt reality was simple: ecosystems are much better at delivering choice and flexibility—the new basis of competition. A bevy of different types of organizations with a broad range of capabilities can respond much more quickly to changing market needs than a single organization, vertically integrated, with a smaller set of capabilities.

What Dean recognized is what other telco executives are realizing: that telcos can become part of a thriving ecosystem of services featuring choice and flexibility. How is this playing out? Telephone application program interfaces (APIs) are trying to lock their customers in voice and data plans. Once customers are in these plans, the company that manages the plan becomes the foundation for the multiple data services and applications delivered. Second, telcos also recognize that the vertical integration model is no longer relevant. Telcos consist of three distinct sets of services: access, connectivity, and distribution. Recognizing that these different sets of services exist and that different types of organizations are better at some of these than others puts the traditional telco in a new role: that of orchestrating the very different capabilities that these services represent to capture the new sources and amounts of value within mobile computing.

Ecosystem Engines of Value Creation—
Network Effects and Lock-In

It's instructive to note that Apple's operating system—iOS—and Google's Android have become focal points for service creation and distribution; it's intriguing as well to recognize that in the space of five years they have created as much value as it took the telcos nearly thirty years to build. How? They orchestrated a set of capabilities that customers wanted and were willing to pay for; they catalyzed ecosystems of services and applications that rested on the carrier transmission capabilities of telcos while at the same time executing a powerful jujitsu move (a martial arts in which you use the strength of your opponent to your advantage) in the industry to radically shift and capture new sources of value.

Apple, Google, and Facebook catalyzed these new sources of value. They became the gravitational force of a new ecosystem, connecting the core business of the telco (the carrier pipes) or the platform owner (hardware and devices for Apple) with an array of capabilities, such as developers, media brands, and service providers critical to meeting the new needs these capabilities afforded in a way that customers were willing to pay for. In short, the ecosystem added even more value to the core products while the new types of organizations and new customers grew around it. By so doing, these companies highlighted what underlies ecosystem economics: network effects and customer lock-in.

The term *network effects* describes a phenomenon whereby a good or service becomes more valuable as more people use it. As more people use Facebook, based on its premise of "connecting the world," it becomes easier—and more valuable—for you to see who else you are connected to in that world.

Lock-in describes the process of you continuing to use what you are using because the costs to change outweigh the benefits of changing. For example, iPhone apps attract millions of Apple users who, in turn, attract more developers who make more apps, which attract even more users. As you get familiar with some of these apps, it becomes more costly and difficult to start using others that perform a similar purpose; you get locked-in to using the apps you already have.

Network effects and lock-in are complementary sides of the same coin, an image that helps us understand ecosystem economics. The network effect between developers and users drives the explosive growth of the iOS platform. Lock-in creates natural walled gardens as users develop habits around specific applications they use again and again. Simultaneously developers get locked-in because of the high cost it would take to leave the current iOS system they have invested in and work in.

Here it gets particularly interesting: physics has a concept that helps explain how order emerges out of complexity—*strange attractors*. Strange attractors represent an element or force around which other activities and elements coalesce in a recognizable, repeatable pattern. For example, Saturn's rings consist of millions of different sizes and shapes of dust and rocks. The gravity that holds them together is a strange attractor because it creates a recurring pattern—the rings—out of fast-moving and seemingly unconnected elements. Strange attractors have been used to make hidden relationships among seemingly chaotic activities—ranging from measles outbreaks and financial contagion to flood patterns and quantum computing—visible. Strange attractors explain the different types and shapes of the various business ecosystems.

If you replace the phrase *strange attractors* with that of *control points*, you can start to see how network effects and customer lock-in support ecosystem economics. Let's take a look at how.

Control Points

Control points are sets of capabilities around which new sources of value are catalyzed and grow. This value is primarily based on meeting customers' unmet needs and overcoming customer friction. For each of these the question is, What are the critical control points around which any new feature will be orchestrated to unlock, or claim, the value?

The control points for mobile computing are content creation and distribution. Content must be relevant to customers to motivate them to consume it—whether it's a best seller, a viral video, an elegant financial model, or a compelling mobile game. Locking developers into a proprietary API they develop content for and locking customers into an API their content is accessed from becomes a critical control point—the strange attractor—around which mobile computing ecosystems get orchestrated.

Content is useless, of course, unless it is consumed; it is impossible to consume unless it gets distributed. Consequently, distribution becomes an equally critical control point to bring about and capture new sources of value. For mobile computing, platform owners control content distribution by gating how apps are distributed to or discovered by end users. Strong and proprietary APIs amplify network effects by reducing the friction of onboarding developers and users. Those who own the customer relationship via simple, seamless distribution amplify lock-in. Both provide the strange attractors around which features are used to create value. This gives platform owners a huge voice in terms of how value gets distributed throughout their ecosystem.

Just look at iTunes. This platform shifted the allocation of value for music purchased away from the artists, and even the studio that produced and owned the music, to those who distributed it, namely Apple—even as iTunes created enormous new sources and amounts of value in music streaming.

Back to Dean and telcos. The teasing apart of the mobile and telco business services into access, connectivity, and distribution was inevitable—the result of technological advances. One implication? A significant shift in how value gets allocated to these different areas. Another? A change in the competitive game.

Connectivity is a game of scale and commoditization. The reason telcos around the world are merging into larger and larger players simply reflects that the connectivity game is a commodity one, requiring playing the scale game as quickly and as aggressively as possible. Margins are always under pressure in any commoditized game. No scale? No growth.

Because connectivity costs are paid by the end user, the OTT players and content creators have more flexibility in terms of what they can do, the prices they can charge, and the margins they can realize. They can monetize ads, downloads, and analytics, as well as price their services free (think Viber), closer to free (WhatsApp, Candy Crush), or less than free. Telcos can't play here; they have been forced to play at a different services layer. The point here is not that they don't have room to maneuver. It does mean, however, that (a) they are part of a broader ecosystem than they were before and (b) there is a need to think through how to engage within these ecosystems as they rethink what control points they must work through to catalyze new sources of value.

Section Summary: Value Seen Is Value Captured

W. Brian Arthur is a US national treasure. He is a physicist, a professor, and one of America's brilliant minds, with some of his awards including the Lagrange Prize in Complexity Science and a Guggenheim Fellowship. He teaches at the Santa Fe Institute, a research and academic center focused on understanding the science of complexity and emerging models of computing.[36] His research focuses on the economy and business as interconnected systems that adapt to the many millions of daily decisions and actions taken by firms and individuals within them.

An economy, he states, is a set of arrangements and activities a society uses to fulfill its needs.[37] A business is an organization that orchestrates its capabilities to meet them. It adapts based on a repeatable algorithm (set of steps) that he describes:

1. A novel technology appears. It is created from particular existing ones, and enters the business, or economy, as a novel element.
2. The novel element becomes available to replace existing technologies and business practices.

---

36   Santa Fe Institute homepage, http://www.santafe.edu, accessed December 29, 2015.
37   W. Brian Arthur, *Complexity and the Economy* (New York: Oxford University Press, 2014): 19.

3. The novel element sets up further needs or *opportunity niches* around which the business focuses and restructures its organizational arrangements.
4. The business and economy, defined as the pattern of goods and services produced and consumed, readjust to these steps. Costs and prices, and therefore incentives for even more novel technologies, change accordingly.

Arthur illustrates this algorithm using the following example:

> The railway locomotive was constructed from the already-existing steam engine, boiler, cranks, and iron wheels. It entered the collected economy around 1829 (1); replaced existing horse-drawn trains (2); set up needs for the fabrication of iron rails and the organization of railways (3); caused the canal and horse-drayage industries to wither (4); became a key component in the transportation of goods (5); and in time caused prices and incentives across the economy to change (6). Such events may operate in parallel . . .[38]

As this algorithm plays out, it begins a sequence of events that never end, because each triggers a cascade of further events. This sounds like what we already well know: businesses evolve, and they need to adapt to their competitive environment.

But there's a difference in Arthur's approach, two wrinkles that further demonstrate the importance of taking a system-based ecosystem perspective.

First, what emerges from the continual adaptions is "an ecology of strategies, each attempting to exploit and survive" within their ecosystem. This system of novel technologies calls forth or demands further technologies—e.g., data storage, languages, computational algorithms,

---

38   Ibid.

or social platforms. These technologies in turn demand further technologies. A novel technology is never a one-time insertion into an existing business or technology environment but a permanent ongoing generator and demander of further technologies.

We see this clearly as new technology platforms get introduced, as in the steam engine, the transistor, the web, multi-modal reality, machine learning, and cognitive technologies. New ways to make sense and take action open up to create and destroy value. Even well-positioned businesses get nibbled at as new entrants from different SIC codes blur the boundaries of their traditional market opportunities.

Second, ecosystems reflect the consequences of interactions among different businesses and organizations. An analysis of patterns of activities that emerge from interactions among various organizations provides foresight into where value is likely to emerge—or to disappear. An ecosystem perspective provides insight into how these changes are likely to play out.

> Viewing your business from an ecosystem perspective helps reveal the way change is propagated through interconnected behavior— how activities impact each other.

When a bank comes under stress, it may pass this change to its connected neighbors, which may pass it to their neighbors, which pass it on to theirs, and on and on. Decisions cause ripple effects. Systemic risk, which we all became far too aware of after the Global Financial Crisis of 2007, is a blunt example of the ripple effects that can occur across geographies, businesses, and people.

Arthur suggests that it is critical to recognize that patterns exist regarding how technologies arise and enter the economy and our businesses. These patterns create and recreate a mutually new set of interactions that structurally affect the economy and the business models that comprise it. Business ecosystems are no more than the new set of interactions that have arisen and are becoming the new engines of both growth and value creation. Identifying the type of business ecosystem that's relevant for you allows you to take advantage of Arthur's insight into the adaptive algorithm that powers economic growth.

Types of Business Ecosystems

Different types of business ecosystems allocate value differently. For example, Airbnb, Apple, and Goldman Sachs reflect one type of business ecosystem—that of market maker. They control how value is allocated throughout their ecosystem. Think about it. What is surge pricing by Uber, other than a reflection of their capability to set prices, thereby stimulating more supply to meet demand? Their market dominance allows them not only to set prices for their customers but also to determine how much to pay their drivers. Uber has been accused by drivers of squeezing the amount they pay them over time. Other models, that we call the speculator models, share risk and reward across their players. For example, Hotels.com and Priceline share the money they make based on the unused inventory—e.g., hotel rooms, plane tickets—they are able to sell.

Different types of business ecosystems, different ways of allocating risk and distributing value throughout them. Insight into how value is distributed across an ecosystem provides one more consideration as you explore which model is more or less relevant to you.

JAXA is one of the most important Japanese agencies that few have ever heard of. They produce a smart piece of equipment—small, yes, but critical. It has been called the *brain stem* orchestrating radar guidance in many airplanes and helicopters as well as a large percentage of missiles and other airborne products. Without it, the rest of the airborne products cannot be, well, in the air. Consequently, it is a critical *control point* that determines the financial market value of its surrounding products. JAXA performs a critical role within its ecosystem, requiring many of the other different types of firms within its air products ecosystem to be tied to it. Using Arthur's terms, it has created foundational novel elements that trigger new innovations, both technically (to develop it) and organizationally (to deliver it). Cisco's refocus on standards and architectural design is another critical control point around which its ecosystem is designed and value gets allocated. Boeing's rests on its capabilities to orchestrate thousands of suppliers around its requirements. Amazon's Alexa focuses around the APIs it's building to support a new wave of buying . . . just about anything.

Value in any ecosystem gets allocated according to the critical control points that other capabilities from different types of businesses mobilize around. You want to engage in connected cities? Figure out how to take advantage of Cisco's architectural designs and standards. You want to become part of Uber's economy? Simply use their app and start driving. You want to take advantage of voice and augmented reality commerce? Figure out how to use Alexa's or Google Home's APIs. Where you end up playing will require figuring out what the control points are where (a) other capabilities get orchestrated and (b) value gets allocated.

Value captured is value seen. This truism comes sharply in focus when you look at the explosive growth rates of some entrepreneurial companies that have identified and monetized sources of value that others had either not seen or ignored.

Why an ecosystem perspective? Because no one—neither person nor business, neither product nor service—exists in isolation. We are all embedded in a tapestry, an ecosystem of different actors, actions, activities, currencies, services, and product flows. We must ask how to make sense of our ecosystems and monetize them to our advantage.

This section explored key elements underlying value from an ecosystem perspective:

- New foundations of value—regarding where to focus
- The new 20 percent of capabilities critical to capturing them—regarding how to focus
- The half-life of assets—regarding the sustainability of your capabilities

- Control points—regarding mechanisms to orchestrate distinctive value
- The concept of currencies—regarding what types of value to create when, to whom, and with whom
- A shared value framework—regarding how to mobilize different types of stakeholders around a common objective
- TEO—regarding the amount of the potential impact, making visible what is typically invisible

However, none of this matters unless we understand new ways to engage customers, given our changed competitive landscapes. As Peter Drucker, the fabled business strategist, once put it, no customers, no business. As we've said many times before, technologies advance. Customer expectations change. And business models innovate. These all need to fit together. But none of them will take off unless we heed Drucker's sage advice. No customers, no business—hence the tremendous focus on customer experience and customer centricity.

But, much like we've already seen, an ecosystem perspective shifts how we make sense of the new opportunities ahead of us. How does this perspective change—and challenge—our insights and, most importantly, our actions regarding how we engage with customers? This is the focus of the next section.

New Ways to Engage Your. Customers

Jared Carver is chief strategy officer and a general manager at Converse. Converse is a hipster company. Its Chuck Taylor sneakers remain a staple in many closets. Not known for its physical comfort, the Chuck Taylor for decades has instead provided psychic comfort based on its eclectic and extensive range of styles. These styles speak to a wide range of customer segments and ages across generations. From Superman and celebrity designs to vibrant-colored patterns and the classic black-and-white logo, Converse shoes have remained iconic symbols of style and self-expression. Yet even for them, markets move and customer requirements change, making them susceptible to changes in what they do and how they do it.

Converse was acquired by Nike in 2003 to complement Nike's already enormous footprint. Nike, arguably *the* preeminent sports clothing brand, sought to strengthen its positioning as a style company through its acquisition of Converse.[39] Recently, Converse's revenue growth has slowed, although its margins have remained strong.[40] A strategic refocus was needed to both reignite Converse's growth and figure out how to add measurable value to the Nike empire.

Jared, along with Converse's chief marketing officer (CMO), thought of revamping their market positioning tagline for two reasons. First, to indicate that Converse was going to start focusing on comfort as well as style. Second, to align with the broader market positioning that Nike held. A new tagline was "Made to move." Clarifying what "Made to move" meant from existing and potential consumers' perspectives would have had striking implications—as much for Converse's management as for its consumers. This idea reflected a common trend across many product companies. Let's explore this common trend and how it leads to the imperative to engage with customers in new ways.

What do Schneider Electric, BMW, Tesla, Merck, Coca-Cola, Nike, and Chamberlain have in common? They are all product companies trying to figure out how to provide more services. Nike's extension of their business to support personalized design of their shoes for their customers is an example of this. You can go to Nike.com, select a type of shoe you want, and personalize it: colors, type of laces, and imagery on the shoe. The intent? More flexible ways to engage with customers. Schneider Electric has moved toward offering air compression as a service; you can purchase the amount of air compressed rather than the air compressor itself. Their per-usage pricing arrangement reflects what Schneider Electric heard that their customers wanted—namely, more flexible fee schedules. It also tapped into a broader business trend toward per-usage fees and servicing arrangements with customers.

39   Steve Symington of the Motley Fool, "This is Nike's Secret Weapon," CNN Money, Apr. 8, 2015, http://money.cnn.com/2015/04/08/investing/nike-secret-weapon-converse/.

40   "Revenue of Converse Worldwide from 2010 to 2016 (in Million US Dollars)," Statistica.com, accessed June 30, 2017, https://www.statista.com/statistics/241850/sales-of-nikes-non-nike-brands-2006-2010/.

The implications of allowing your customers to customize their products or services or even creating a usage-based pricing program involve organizational activities beyond doing more of the same, only better, faster, and cheaper. It involves *doing different*—engaging with customers in new ways. Doing so entails the development and use of a different set of capabilities underlying your employees, pricing models, and channels. In short, services are a different game than products.

Back to Converse.

The "Made to move" tagline highlighted a call to interact with their consumers differently. These differences would have involved more than drawing customers into a store and offering them a broad array of style options. It would have involved even more than what Nike offered in terms of the capability for consumers to customize their shoes.

The "Made to move" campaign carried other characteristics if you unpack the concept: customization, sure, that's the "made" part of the tagline. But "to move" included movement from two more perspectives:

- **Physical.** This perspective would have required a new focus on comfort to complement the Chuck Taylor style. This would have been a striking change for any of us who had proudly worn our less-than-comfortable Chuck Taylors.

- **Psychic.** This tapped into the perspective of those who select Converse shoes as a statement, including those who select the shoes reflecting their hipster or other personal statements of style.[41]

Either and both would require as much attention to what services meant for Converse as did product design and manufacturing. Either and both would require new ways of engaging their customers.

---

41   "Category Killers: E-Commerce Startups Disrupting Brick-and-Mortar Brands," CBInsights, November 3, 2015, https://www.cbinsights.com/research/category-killer-ecommerce-startups/.

Section Road Map

This section explores new ways of engaging customers from an ecosystem perspective. It consists of two chapters that tease apart key considerations of what this entails and how these considerations point to different steps to take to catalyze new sources of value.

Chapter 5 explores the ever-increasing focus on customer experience. Without doubt, this focus is critical for both consumer-based and business-to-business companies—driven by both changing customer expectations ("since my experience is great in my personal life, it should be equally simple and great in my work life") and technological advances, which drive these expectations.

However, here's a question for you: If everyone is moving toward greater customer experience, then what will be a sustainable advantage for you over time? Here's another: What does customer experience actually mean? And whose perspective does it typically refer to? And finally, how does an ecosystem perspective help you answer these questions differently than is typically done?

Without doubt, customer experience and customer centricity are critical: the first to focus on and the second as an execution principle. However, our focus is to suggest how to capture explosive rather than incremental growth. This section suggests how insights from new business models, powered by business ecosystems, help you do so.

Chapter 6 suggests how rethinking traditional approaches to customer centricity, from an ecosystem perspective, has implications for new ways to engage customers, and the business models that underlie explosive growth.

5

Customer Experience, from Whose Perspective?

Alex Malorodov, in the summer of 2015, distilled lessons from a subset of extremely fast-growing, new market entrants in the consumer products industry—including Bonobos, Casper, Dollar Shave Club, Harry's, and Warby Parker—companies that have grown from unknown start-ups to leading brands in their respective categories. He profiled the characteristics of these high-growth companies, seeking to distill patterns of potential use for other companies in terms of which elements they mobilized around (their new 20 percent). We'll highlight elements of his profile that reflected how these companies engaged their customers and how that engagement catalyzed their explosive growth.[42]

Customer Experience—an Explosive Growth Engine?

All of these companies targeted specific market needs, serviced by a highly concentrated group of companies; more than 50 percent of the market had been controlled by four or fewer incumbents. All of the incumbents

---

42   "Category Killers: E-Commerce Startups Disrupting Brick-and-Mortar Brands," CBInsights, November 3, 2015, https://www.cbinsights.com/research/category-killer-ecommerce-startups/.

characterized themselves as product companies. They generally enjoyed high margins, which, given the degree to which they dominated the market, tended to translate into a relatively high degree of price control. They also all tended to rely on different types of distribution channels, which reflected sunk costs that made it difficult to lower prices and still maintain the margins they enjoyed. There were clearly specific areas of friction in each of these markets, and the new high-growth companies homed in on these areas aggressively, recognizing that reducing friction was their way to capture new sources of value quickly and at scale.

Each of the high-growth companies shared a common profile tackling the friction inherent in their respective markets of focus. First, each offered a product that was a recurring need for each of the customers. For examples, Warby Parker's glasses and Harry's razors, for those who need to see and those who need to shave, are both products that consumers don't need to be sold on. You either needed to see and shave or you didn't. That created a clear (and large) universe of potential customers. This allowed the new entrants to perform a beautiful jujitsu move—using the strength of the incumbents against themselves, thereby shifting where the value would be articulated and the competitive game played. Second, they focused on wrapping the products they offered with *services*, aiming extreme and detailed attention on the type of *experience* that the customers had, to date, lacked.

For example, Harry's products, whether the basic razor, its blades, or its more expansive set of grooming products, come in a finely designed, richly colored and textured box. They, along with Warby Parker's and a number of the other companies, focused on the "magic moment" of unboxing the product, designed to create a memorable experience. As Malorodov writes, "It is not an accident that YouTube is filled with thousands of . . . unboxing videos." They also curated (to use a fancy term of the day that simply means paid lots of attention to) a set of services and experiences to cater to each customer in a highly personalized and flexible way. Harry knew which products you purchased and when you did so. They certainly knew—and know—how long products tended to last. And so they would reach out via email, phone call, or text message—however you engaged them—to ask if there was anything else they might do to help you "make your experience and the product" more useful.

The focus on experience and service—filling out a tapestry made up of product, services, and experience-based capabilities—was no accident. The focus on experience—whether the magic unboxing moments or the personalized outreach from so-called concierges or experience catalysts—gets customers to recommend the company as a whole. One telling YouTube reviewer who did not like the product still recommended the company to others because, he said, both the service and experience realized were so positive. This further emphasizes the criticality of rounding out how you engage your customers.

One more attribute to highlight ties back to parts of our value discussion in Section 1, particularly the concept of currencies. Currencies, as a reminder, are different types of value that matter—and motivate—different people to act. Embedding a component of social good into the value proposition of some of these high-growth companies—for example, Warby Parker's "Buy a Pair, Give a Pair," whereby they donate a pair of glasses to someone who cannot afford them each time a customer buys one—bolsters brand affinity and helps to support the "triple bottom line" that underpins a number of shared value frameworks. It also highlights the emerging positioning and orchestration of capabilities that business ecosystems enable—namely, that some of these business models are premised on creating both greater economic value *and* societal benefit. The "cost" of delivering on this proposition can be distributed across—or borne by—some of the different actors involved in the ecosystem, depending on what motivates them.

The focus on customer experience is, of course, "good business sense." But it's more than that. It is a lens to get insight into the changing economics of where value is allocated throughout an ecosystem, why industry structures are shifting, and consequently how new business models are being created to take advantage of these changes.

The Economics of Customer Experience and
the Bundling/Unbundling of Industries

Davide Grasso, Converse's CEO, is extremely passionate about creating an exceptional customer experience. Converse, after all, is a company whose value proposition rests on delivering self-expression. And Jim Calhoun, Converse's previous CEO, demonstrating continuity in their focus, once stated that "celebrating the authentic and being different [for our customers] is the center of what we do and what we hold precious."[43] This is no surprise to anyone. The past twenty years have seen a tsunami of focus and resources spent on getting closer to customers and of building new capabilities and processes to do so. Forrester, an industry research group, is mobilizing much of its research and analyst time on the customer—recognizing that sustainable value for any company will only be realized by supporting the customer.[44] So far our only response is "of course".

But what are the implications of this focus on where and how value is allocated within and across industry boundaries? This is where the concept of bundling and unbundling comes in.

Previously, we discussed Marc Andreessen and Jim Barksdale's reflections that there are only two types of businesses: those that bundle and those that unbundle capabilities. Bundle is merely a fancy word for integrating a wide range of capabilities that all organizations need—from making products to distributing, selling, and servicing or supporting them. In business terms, the more organizations bundle, the more vertically integrated they are—i.e., the more they own the capabilities and internalize the costs of their execution. Unbundle is merely a fancy word for the opposite; capabilities are modular, owned and executed by different firms, with the costs of execution—from making to servicing products or services—distributed across those who provide them.

Market cycles tend to see greater or lesser bundling and unbundling. At its extreme form, the concerns about "too big to fail" of the largest banks in the world reflect a concern that these enormous, vertically

---

43   Discussion with Jim Calhoun, January 10, 2016.
44   Discussion with George Colony, CEO of Forrester Research, January 9, 2016.

integrated firms internalize risks far too much, creating an enormous society-wide risk should they fail. From this perspective, unbundling some key capabilities of these institutions would distribute risk across a far greater number of players, thus building in a resilience when we face another financial crisis. We use this as a quick example of what we mean by the bundling or unbundling of organizational capabilities.

So why bundle and why unbundle? We explored this a bit in Chapter 2 in terms of how bundling and unbundling are driven by the sets of capabilities different actors bring to the table. Here we look at it from a customer-experience perspective. Specifically, we explore how the economics of customer experience shape where and how bundling and unbundling is happening and will happen across industries, further evidence of the need for new business models powered by the new strategic questions. Ben Thompson, an insightful technology analyst, put it:

> The Internet has . . . transformed business by making both distribution and transaction costs effectively free [for digital goods] . . . this has . . . changed the calculus when it comes to adding new customers: specifically, it is now possible to build a business where every incremental customer has both zero marginal costs and zero opportunity costs.[45]

This is a straightforward observation with profound implications. Instead of some companies servicing the high end of a market, providing customers a superior experience while others serve a lower-end customer base, delivering a *good-enough* experience, one company can serve everyone. This distinction between high and low end reflects not only the market segmentation we have had for years but an explanatory entry point for new players to disrupt any particular market.

Recall that Clayton Christensen's theory of disruption is based on new market entrants that target customers who are either underserved

45 Ben Thompson, "Beyond Disruption," Stratechery, December 2, 2015,
    https://stratechery.com/2015/beyond-disruption/.

because they are insufficiently profitable or nonserved because the price points of engaging them are too high. In either case, the new entrant—the disruptor—makes, distributes, sells, and services a good-enough product that the incumbent is likely to ignore, because the marginal costs of servicing that lower end of the market are too great; it isn't worth it.

But when the marginal costs of customer acquisition fall dramatically, does this change the game? And, to that end, if a customer is given the choice between realizing there is a superior experience and one that is good enough, which one will they go for? The superior customer experience, of course. Wouldn't you?

That's what we're seeing underlying a number of the explosive-growth companies; it is also why we are seeing a blurring among product, service, and experience from all types of organizations, whether product or service companies. It is also why customer experience becomes arguably *the* critical control point—to get insight into not only what the customer wants but also how to orchestrate different capabilities critical to delivering extraordinary customer experience. Peter Thiel, the venture capitalist and cofounder of eBay and PayPal, believes businesses should go big or go home. New businesses and the ecosystems they orchestrate need to have an end game of owning the entire market. Otherwise, why bother?[46]

From this perspective, taking the classic disruption innovator pathway of providing good-enough services to an underserved market and then building up and into incumbent space is not necessary, particularly where the marginal costs of customer acquisition are practically zero. And people are willing to pay for extraordinary design and experience, compared to good-enough products (merely observe the number of people willing to shell out well over $600 for the iPhone compared to others). It makes sense, accordingly, to start at the high end of a market with customers who have a greater willingness to pay and scale downward, decreasing your price along with the decrease in your per-customer cost base as you go.

---

46   Peter Thiel, *Zero to One: Notes on Startups, or How to Build the Future* (New York: Crown, 2014).

Who does this sound like? Maybe Uber? Ben Thompson reminds us:

> [Uber] spent its early years building its core technology and delivering a high-end experience with significantly higher prices than incumbent taxi companies. Eventually, though, *the exact same technology* was deployed to deliver a lower-priced experience to a significantly broader customer base.[47]

He continues:

> Google, Facebook, Amazon, Netflix, Snapchat, Uber, Airbnb and more [have followed this same model,] delivering a superior experience that begins at the top of a market and works its way down until they have aggregated consumers, giving them leverage over their suppliers and the potential to make outsized profits.[48]

The distinction between up-market and down-market is, from a cost basis and the marginal cost of acquisition, increasingly nonexistent. Each of the companies mentioned in this paragraph had what in common? A sharp focus on delivering extraordinary customer experience. They started with a specific customer need around which they mobilized heavily—recognizing that delivering extraordinary customer experience would, as it did, become *the* critical differentiator (i.e., people would be more than happy to pay a premium) and choke point or barrier to entry for anyone else attempting to enter their space. It became, as well, the foundation from which they could expand their capabilities, begin to control how value would be allocated throughout their ecosystem, and, following Peter Thiel's advice, "become *the* market makers." They followed a similar playbook—on tackling a specific point of friction from the customer's perspective—and growing from there.

---

47 Ben Thompson, "The FANG Playbook," Stratechery.com, Jan. 20, 2016, https://stratechery.com/2016/the -fang-playbook/.

48 Ibid.

It's worth reemphasizing a critical point here, one that cannot be overemphasized.

This is not your typical focus on customer experience—in terms of identifying pain points that your customer has with respect to how they engage with your existing set of products and services.

Instead, it starts with planting a flag around specific points of friction or customer need and mobilizing different capabilities to meet them. This reflects an outside-in *starting point—from a consumer friction and market need perspective—rather than an* inside-in *perspective based on the current kit of products and services you already have.*

With this in mind, let's look at a quick synopsis of this explosive growth playbook across companies we all know about.

- **Uber:** This ride-sharing pioneer tackled the friction point of inconvenience and lack of transparency. How many times have you ever called a cab and they didn't come, or you were told they were coming but had no insight into precisely when they would arrive? Uber created an easy application to use with a simple visualization to track where your car was and when it would get to you. Surge pricing? Sure, we tend to be more than happy to pay it for the convenience and ease of use—the friction reduction—it enables.

- **Amazon:** The company originally sold books and held no inventory. Amazon would order the book you requested once you placed an order and then ship it to you using preexisting parcel shippers. They added an entry point—a portal into a vast selection of books, more than any offline bookstore could provide, at lower prices. Why buy from anyone/anywhere else?

- **Google:** Google didn't create any of the pages accessible through its search engine. Nor did it take you directly to the content of those pages. Its algorithm mapped to the link rather than the content, thereby providing a radically easier and faster way to find what you were looking for.

- **Facebook:** The company tackled a simple problem, initially: connect me to friends within a preexisting network and make it radically simple to do so. The friction it tackled and the customer experience it supported hasn't changed. It is relentlessly focused on doing more of the same, just at a larger scale.

All of these companies have the same message: it is all about the quality of the experience and the capability to scale. Use customer as the new *control point* of differentiation and you become the allocator of value. This has become possible because of the Internet and the complementary technologies that ride on it. And this is where and how the new models of business ecosystems come back into the picture.

Bundling and Unbundling for Customer Engagement

Netscape's Andreessen is cited frequently for saying that "software eats industries." Put differently, what software does—more specifically, the Internet and the digital technologies of mobile, social, and the cloud—is reallocate how value is distributed across the make, distribute, sell, and service stages, the ever-recurring, never-going-away sets of capabilities that make up every value chain. From this perspective, the question is less "to bundle or not to bundle" than it is "what, when, and how to bundle and unbundle." And here is where looking at some of the Internet giants and some of the explosive new business ecosystems becomes instructive. We'll do so by focusing on where and why the control points of value have shifted and the implications for business models and customer engagement.

In the pre-Internet era, distribution was a critical control point for capturing value. It was difficult to establish the economies of scale to get products to consumers. Consequently, significant effort was spent on building robust distribution channels around which value could be controlled. For example, printed newspapers were the primary means of distributing content to consumers in a given geographic region. They used this distribution as a choke point to integrate backward into content creation—i.e., the supplier of content—and earned significant profits through the delivery of advertising. It was similar in the taxi market. Taxis owned dispatch—i.e., distribution—and controlled how value was allocated by owning the asset—i.e., the content to be consumed—as measured, and controlled, by the taxi medallion. Hotels also bundled the assets (the rooms to be provided) with their distribution channels (namely, their brands). In each of these industries, the distributors bundled—or integrated—backward into supply. In an environment where there were more users or consumers than suppliers and transactions were costly, owning the supplier relationship provided leverage—e.g., you could manage the supply/demand balance and hence the pricing power.

Digital technologies have changed this, starting with the Internet as the foundation on which the other technologies sit. First, the Internet has made the distribution of digital goods (nearly) free, dramatically decreasing the value of distribution which distributors leveraged to integrate with suppliers. Second, the Internet has made transaction costs nearly zero, creating a fundamental shift to integrate forward with the end consumers at scale.

Bundling capabilities forward means shifting focus toward providing extraordinary customer service and experience. The critical choke point shifts, then, from being a distributor (involving lock-in with back-end suppliers) to customer experience. Why? Because that is where, disproportionately, the new value is being created. This is why the telco providers have been so nervous about the way OTT providers have been effective in positioning their carriers as the commodity distributors of connectivity. The carriers clearly benefit from the OTT relationships, which have been instrumental in increasing data usage, thereby reducing the jaws chart lines between voice and data. However, the customer experience relationship accrues to the OTT or app players with a stark competitive and positioning implication: the carriers become commoditized suppliers forced to compete on scale, given the ever-increasing pressures on margins and price. Meanwhile, those companies that provide the customer experience compete on scale, sure, but one based on brand loyalty and apparently ever-increasing willingness to pay premium prices for the experience. "Keep my Candy Crush, irrespective of what carrier network it sits on!"

The game has changed. No longer do distributors compete based on exclusive supplier relationships. Instead, suppliers can be aggregated at scale, which makes consumers the primary focus, hence the focus on customer centricity. Products and services will come and go. But delivering extraordinary customer experience will support premium prices and allow you to go down-market easier. Ben Thompson summarizes:

> By extension, this means that the most important factor determining success is the user experience: the best distributors/aggregators/market-makers win by providing the best experience, which earns them the most consumers/users, which attracts the most suppliers, which enhances the user experience in a virtuous cycle.[49]

Previous incumbents, whether newspapers, book publishers, telecommunications carriers, taxi companies, or hospital providers, integrated backward to "own" their supply chain and lost value in favor of those who bundled forward with the consumer and who now have a near exclusive relationship with them.

Recall the stories of these businesses:

- **Airbnb:** Previously, the value proposition hotels held was based on their trust in their brand; you wanted a particular type of experience, and based on what you were willing to pay, you assumed you would get a similar experience for the brand you were looking for, whether you stayed at the Ritz, Marriott, or Days Inn. They

---

49   Ben Thompson, "Aggregation Theory," Stratechery.com, July 21, 2015, https://stratechery.com/2015/aggregation-theory/.

integrated vacant rooms and sought to encourage you to stay with
them based on their inventory and their brand. Airbnb changed
this. They unbundled vacant properties, building a reputation system for trust between hosts and guests, significantly lowering the
relevance of parts of the value chain.

- **Uber:** Previously, taxi companies integrated dispatch and fleet
management. Uber unbundled fleet management by working with
independent drivers, integrating dispatch and customer management with a focus on providing a simple, friction-free experience.
By so doing, they shifted value toward the front, far away from the
back end of the value of owning a medallion.

- **Netflix:** Previously, networks integrated broadcast availability and
content purchases. Netflix unbundled availability by making its
entire library available at any time in any order. They integrated
content purchases with customer experience, enabling a virtuous
cycle of increased subscription demand and increased content
purchase capability.

Three Lessons Stem from This Discussion

Scale used to be driven by control of the distribution channel. When
this was the case, it made sense to own your own assets to push through
these channels. Owning the distribution channel was a critical, competitive barrier to entry: owning a medallion (for taxis), the brand of trust (for
hotels), the underlying connectivity (for telecommunication carriers), or
studios (for films) became the pipes through which content had to flow
and customer experience was mediated. It was similar, in a way, to Henry
Ford's decision to provide everyone with a car, a black one—because that
was what he produced. Those who controlled the distribution channel
and the asset would deliver to profitable customers, whereby profitability
was determined by the control of distribution and the underlying assets
of the company.

First: Where High-Margin Scale Will Come From

Scale is now driven by delivering exceptional customer experience and the insight gained from aggregating those experiences into what matters to customers—what they want to do, what they are willing to spend, and their behavioral patterns in how they use the products and services, which provides yet more insight and thereby more fuel for delivering even greater experience. Quite the virtuous cycle.

Given this model, the customer now has nearly infinite access to products necessary to support what it is they need or want. So it's logical that the new firms, and their underlying models, don't own many, if any, of the assets they aggregate to deliver to customers. Reflecting what? A dramatic unbundling and rebundling of one's value chain, typically (always?) pulling capabilities from other industries.

Second: Why the Economics of Customer Experience Have Changed

Integrating forward from distribution, or orchestrating different products and services, with a crisp focus on delivering exceptional customer experience, captures new sources of value—particularly in a world where the marginal costs of customer acquisition and distribution are (nearly) zero. The new competitive barrier or control point, then, becomes the delivery of exceptional customer experience, from the perspective of the jobs customers want to do and the ecosystems in which they spend their time, money, and energy.

This explains why a number of companies are expanding to deliver the types of services their customers want them to—irrespective of the SIC code they were once in. A car is a vehicle to get from point A to point B. Previously the driving experience from point A to point B is what separated the great from the good-enough car company. From the perspective of a customer and their "jobs to be done" perspective, enhancing the experience to include data services (to support communications and work activities) and voice-activated concierge services (to support activities to be done) are simple examples of what moving from a *car* to a *mobility* company—where nearly all (formerly known as) automobile companies are repositioning themselves—makes sense. *And is an inevitable foreshadowing of what will happen to other industries around the globe.*

Third: What the Implications Are for New Business Models

The blunt reality is that explosive value is driven by business ecosystems that orchestrate a bundling of products, services, and experiences in new ways. This orchestration is a reflection of a structural economic change within many of today's value chains and helps explain why experience becomes today's new competitive moat or control point. With digital capabilities making both distribution and transaction costs effectively free, it becomes possible to build certain businesses where every incremental customer has both zero marginal costs and zero opportunity costs. This has profound implications: instead of some companies servicing the high end of a market and others the so-called lower end with *good enough* capabilities and experience, everyone can be delivered an extraordinary experience.

OK, So Customer Experience Is Critical. But . . .

Again, why the urgent focus on customer experience? Because the economics of customer acquisition have fundamentally changed, as has the location—the once mighty barrier influencing where value is allocated across your value chain. As Ben Thompson reminds us, "In its proximity to customers, superior user experience, and new business models that simply weren't possible before,"[50] the strategic game has changed—for good.

So the strategic game becomes all about the quality of the experience and capabilities to scale. Fine, at a high level. But dig a bit deeper, and you discover three things. First, the bundling/unbundling process highlights that you do not need (nor definitely want to have) all of the capabilities that you used to have. Which means that identifying the new 20 percent of capabilities critical to capturing your new sources of value becomes a high

---

50   Ibid.

priority. Second, new business models (again, merely a fancy way of saying *methods to orchestrate your resources effectively*) are needed; what made you successful yesterday (or today) will not be what carries you onto the high-impact playing field tomorrow. And third, customer centricity becomes the new control point of value creation and allocation.

And yet.

We have two questions for you. First, if everyone realizes this and folks around the world are investing aggressively and quickly around customer experience and customer centricity, then are we not soon going to run the risk of running the Red Queen race? What *is* different, distinctive, and most importantly sustainable about this focus on customer experience? And second, much as an ecosystem perspective sheds new light on preexisting activities, might not its insights do the same on how we understand what we all know to be the new control point around customer centricity?

The short answer to the first question is an emphatic yes. Expanding this answer a bit—if these initial questions are not of concern to you now, they should be. That people are investing in similar ways will force organizations to run the "we've gotta outexecute everyone else" race. This is a tough race to run over time. It can work, for a while. But it is not sustainable, and it is susceptible to new business models, distinctive insights, and new competitive entrants.

The answer to the second question is answered in the next chapter.

The insight so far? Understand the ecosystem in which your customer engages; mobilize around the new foundations of value that underlie *that* ecosystem; shape the experience in it; control the core sources of value that drive it to shape its downstream allocation; and orchestrate the capabilities from other actors to do so.

Much as an ecosystem perspective sheds new light on how to think about customer experience, it has equally significant implications for how we rethink customer centricity. Let's see how.

6

Beyond Customer Centricity
to Ecosystem Engagement

Know your customer. This has become such a loud rallying cry as to drown out voices pointing out how to actually do so. An extraordinary amount of effort is expended to know one's customer from the perspective of the specific products and services offered to them rather than how or why a customer uses them. So, ironically, much of the effort on customer centricity is actually like viewing the world (of the customer) through the end lens of a telescope: a large opening (of data about the customer) capable of seeing only a very small set of activity, albeit in great detail. Another apt analogy is the blind man and the elephant, with different parts of the elephant representing different sets of data about one's customer. In this analogy, multiple blind men are holding on to different parts of the elephant. One holds an ear, another the tail, another the trunk, and so on. An elephant, says the one holding the tail, is like a stiff broom; the one holding the ear describes the elephant as a piece of fabric waving in the wind; the one holding the trunk describes it as a long column of rippled fabric; and so on. Each is an apt description of a particular part of the elephant (or customer), but all miss the point of what it means to be an elephant (or customer and what they care about).

On the flip side, you need to start somewhere.

Know Your Customer—But Be Aware of Your Perspective

Enter customer segmentation and customer journey maps. Journey maps are visual descriptions of where, when, and how customers tend to interact with you through the products or services you currently provide. They are starting points to get insight into who your customers are and could be.[51] Better maps focus as much on behavioral characteristics of your customers as on their physical and transactional, easily measurable attributes. It has become clear that insight into how your customers, existing and prospective, actually behave provides a more effective predictor of performance than if you assume they will act as they say they will based on similar characteristics of age, industry, income, even life stages[52]. The use of big data and analytics has turned this type of insight into table stakes—something you must do to stay in the competitive game.

Because many companies are wrestling with blurring among products, services, and experiences, there is a need for a different way to gain insight into how to engage the customer, *from their perspective.* This doesn't mean their perspective on how they interact with you or any particular product or service you provide. Instead, it requires a shift of focus on the ecosystem in which *they* engage and what *they* care about.

Clayton Christensen's concept of jobs to be done starts to move in this direction. Focusing on what it is customers want to do, their jobs to be done, and then figuring out how you support these jobs is an effective way to get started.[53] Yet even this perspective remains tied to the starting point of how your existing products and services help customers rather than the starting point of where customers spend their time, energy, and resources—and what *sets* of products and services would be of value to them, irrespective of what products and services you deliver. It is still a

51   Different types of customer journey maps exist. They share a common objective, however. This article summarizes what is similar: Paul Boag, "All You Need to Know about Customer Journey Mapping," SmashingMagazine.com, Jan. 15, 2015, http://www.smashingmagazine.com/2015/01/all-about-customer-journey-mapping/.

52   Scott Magids, Alan Zorfas, and Daniel Leemon, "The New Science of Customer Emotions," HBR.org, Nov. 2015, https://hbr.org/2015/11/the-new-science-of-customer-emotions.

53   Stephen Wunker, Jessica Wattman, and David Farber, *Jobs to Be Done* (New York: AMACOM, 2017).

focus on the small rather than the big end of the telescope. A different and compelling question is, What is it your products and services *afford* your customers to do?

Customer Affordance and Helping Your Customers Do the Jobs They Want to Do

Affordance is an unusual term. It makes us slow down and think through what the interaction between people and the products or technologies they engage entails. Donald Norman, the great user-experience developer from Xerox PARC, introduced the term to explain how products or people *afford* us the opportunity *to do* something with them. Something well designed will make it clear how to interact with it; something poorly designed will not.

For example, when we see a door with a doorknob, we seldom, if ever, think about how to open the door. Its design is intuitive: turn and pull it toward you to open the door. Its design *affords* you the opportunity to know what to do without conscious thought. Have you ever had the experience when standing in front of a door without a doorknob of not knowing how to get through it? You figure it out, of course. But having to think through how to use something means that its design, from Norman's perspective, is neither intuitive nor optimized. There is *friction* in the use of the product.

Such friction has two implications: it serves to irritate the customer or user of the product, and it creates an opportunity for someone to come up with a better design for that product or service. We use the concept of affordance frequently. It is useful to get people to slow down and recognize how their products and services are interacted with by their customers and consequently what new opportunities might exist as a result, from the customer's perspective.

The change to the customer's perspective and, most importantly, to the ecosystem in which they engage is a simple but profound insight with devilishly difficult operational implications for many firms, but a source of extraordinary potential value. This shift is what customer affordance maps illustrate.

Dan Wollenberg, former senior vice president at Chase Bank, the retail arm of JPMorganChase, explains the importance of affordance and an ecosystem perspective:

> It is vital that we shift our focus to the ecosystem in which our customers engage, and what they—not we—care about. People don't want checking accounts, credit cards, bank accounts; they want financial security and the ability to purchase what they want and need, when they want and need to do so . . . We need to learn to shift our focus from how to improve our products and services to what it is customers want to do and how our products and services (and new ones) could help them do that.[54]

A New Use for Customer Segmentation

Customer segmentation provides important insight into different types of customers a company has, or people it hopes to convert into customers. Customer segmentation seeks to identify the most profitable customer a business has and then to direct products and services to them. Its goal, frequently, is to improve retention of the most profitable customers, improve how these customers talk about you positively to other potential high-profitable customers, and build brand loyalty.

The traditional logic here is straightforward.

Because every additional customer accrues a cost to acquire, convert, and maintain, it makes sense to focus on the most profitable customers and to focus segmentation on continuously turning your less-profitable customers into more-profitable ones. Those that aren't profitable can be cut, or you can reduce the cost basis on which you service them. Other

54 Discussion with Dan Wollenberg, January 12, 2017.

organizations will support your less-profitable customers in a way that makes sense—i.e., is profitable—to them. Thus, the process of customer segmentation reflects the segmentation of the market with different types or tiers of organizations serving different types, and segments, of customers. The result? A multitiered market of organizations and customers structured around meeting what is arguably the same market need or customer desire but doing it differently. This reflects the well-structured, multitiered SIC code–based market.

It is also where the role of customer experience, from an ecosystem perspective, comes in and throws a wrench into the works of how we understand customer segmentation and recognize that the traditional logic on which we tend to think about customer experience, centricity, and segmentation is insufficient to drive nonincremental, explosive growth.

How so?

Typical approaches to customer segmentation seek to identify where, when, and how the customer interacts with the business and how to improve the nature of that interaction. Better customer segmentation rests on insight into a customer's behavioral intentions and actions. Such segmentation seeks to learn how someone engages with peers or what their previous engagement patterns are through scraping, collating, and analyzing big data to more effectively exploit small data (as Sarah Diamond of IBM once called it) around specific customers to get them to engage more. However, this focus tends to remain threaded through the lens of your products and services rather than into the jobs or objectives that your customer more broadly cares about.

An ecosystem perspective shifts the focus *from* an inside-out perspective of the business deciding who its customers are and how it can engage them to consume more products and services *to* insight into what can be done to help its customers do the jobs they want to get done in the ecosystem in which they spend their time, money, and energy, irrespective of the products and services the business (currently) provides.

This shift allows us to ask a different set of questions from an ecosystem perspective:

1. Where do our customers spend their time, energy, and money, in terms of the jobs they do or need to do? And what are the friction points, or potential new sources of value, within these ecosystems of engagement?
2. How do our products and services afford, or enable, our customers to meet these needs?
3. What do they not accomplish?
4. What other capabilities (and products/services) are needed to fill in the gaps between what we offer and what the customer needs to do?
5. Who else provides these capabilities?
6. How do we orchestrate them, and what makes up our new 20 percent of capabilities to do so?

This sequence of questions can act as a simple algorithm to structure complexity in a simple way, asking pragmatic questions that lead to profound implications. Try it with any so-called technology or capability. Things that were previously invisible become visible; opportunities previously unknown become knowable—and consequently, possible. Let's see how, by taking an example.

Etihad Airlines: An Example

Etihad Airlines is one of the world's premier airlines. They have won the coveted World's Leading Airline at the World Travel Awards for five consecutive years, including the award for premium customer service in 2015.[55] Prior to the collapse of oil prices to below $50 per barrel, they were also one of the only profitable airlines globally.

James Hogan, Etihad's chairman and CEO, has had a relentless focus on being recognized as the premier airline globally, based on providing

---

55 "Top 100 Airlines in 2017," Skytrax World Airline Awards, accessed December 29, 2015, http://www. worldairlineawards.com/awards/world_airline_rating.html.

extraordinary customer service. He has also held on to an even broader vision for the company: to become the catalyst of travel transformation and an economic foundation of Abu Dhabi as *the* destination of choice for both business customers and retail passengers. Abu Dhabi and its better-known sister city-state, Dubai, have become major airline hubs connecting passengers traveling globally, particularly those traveling to or from Europe or Asia. In 2014, Dubai became the world's busiest airport, with well over 70 million passengers going through its terminals, surpassing London's Heathrow, the second major airport, which had 68 million the same year.[56]

While Dubai has claimed the top spot, powered by Emirates, the Abu Dhabi–based airline Etihad is helping Abu Dhabi become a fast-growing air hub. Etihad distinguishes itself not only by its award-winning passenger service but also by its intent to be to business logistics what Dubai is to passenger pass-through. Abu Dhabi boasts a deepwater port and has invested billions in wide roads and multimodal logistics support: trucks, shipping, trains, air cargo. Etihad has been instrumental to Abu Dhabi's vision as a catalyst of travel transformation and a destination of choice for sophisticated logistics supporting business travel. Consequently, becoming "the global brand of extraordinary airlines service," as James articulates it, consistently involves figuring out how to engage in new ways with both retail and business customers.

Etihad—Lesson #1: Beyond the Table Stakes of Customer Centricity, to Identify Explosive New Sources of Value

Capturing the value around extraordinary airline service requires new ways to engage customers, markets, and stakeholders. Customer segmentation and journey maps provide an expected baseline of customer service. But how do you capture new sources of value that are distinctive,

---

56 "The New World's Busiest International Airport Is . . . ," CNN Staff, Jan 28, 2015, http://www.cnn.com/2015/01/28/travel/busiest-international-airport-2014/.

sustainable, and explosive? (Spoiler alert.) Recall an earlier discussion that explosive value creation stems from tackling customer friction (because either insights or technologies have yet to be pointed here) or market breakdown (because the economics make it difficult to do so).

Focusing on what the market needs, because of nonconsumption or breakdown, rather than what you already do broadens the aperture into explosive new opportunities. How does this work? And how are the lessons of Etihad relevant to you? As we walk through this example, we suggest that you—

- Rethink how an airline—and you—deliver (or can deliver) extraordinary customer experience

- Reimagine where you could plant a flag around customer needs, from their perspective

- Recognize that the new 20 percent of capabilities critical to meeting these goals requires (a) investments and (b) design of a new business model of partners and customers to capitalize on these needs with speed and scale

Airlines are a typical example of an asset-rich product company. Airplanes are expensive, with the Boeing 777 running between $290 and $320 million per plane. Multiply that by a fleet of one hundred airplanes and you carry on your books a large set of assets that need to realize a return. They do so by providing air service to passengers. They have a specific set of operating metrics to measure profitability—including revenue passenger mile (RPM), revenue per available seat mile (R/ASM), and cost per available seat mile (C/ASM). Another "product" they offer is seat space—the amount of square feet passengers occupy, from floor to ceiling, side to side. This seat space is priced and sold dynamically to different types of passengers: first class, business, and economy, with the majority of profitability coming from business-class seats. The battle over premium service stems from the need to protect business-class seats—which is why so many of the long-haul planes, and flights, have proportionately more business-class seat-space than they ever did before.[57]

Premium service from both attendants and plane representatives becomes critical to enhancing passengers' experiences. The better the service, the greater the likelihood that a passenger will become part of the airline's loyalty program and return again.

Yet airlines do not control the *airport* experience. A customer's in-air experience is shaped by their overall travel experience—from arrival, to shopping and waiting lounges and their amenities, through boarding, and ultimately to baggage pickup. All but one US commercial airport is owned and operated by public entities, including local, regional, or state authorities. They hold the keys to this part of the customer journey and the quality of the experience they get. The folks who load and unload your bags? Part of the airport authority. The ones who both prepare and load the food? Part of a food preparation company, such as Food Flying Group or Sodexo. Those who provide security for the airport and the plane? Part of yet another company, like a government service or someone contracted through the airport authority.

The flying experience is already a carefully choreographed ecosystem of different types of companies providing complementary capabilities to maximize the value of each other; poor service from any impacts them all.

James and Etihad knew this well, as certified by the World Airlines Quality awards they had previously won. But James wanted to capture new sources of value. Doing what they were already doing, and doing it better, was of course part of what Etihad was going to do anyway; innovation is always critical for business and incremental growth, important. But *doing different* rather than *doing more of the same* was what Etihad needed. This required James and his company to ask the new strategic

---

57 Daniel Michaels, "Why This Plane Seat Is the Most Profitable," *The Wall Street Journal*, Mar. 4, 2014, http://www.wsj.com/articles/SB10001424052702304585004579418992081321538. And "Despite Return of All-Business-Class Flights, Profit Picture Isn't Taking Off," Apr. 2, 2015, https://www.bizjournals.com/bizjournals/blog/seat2B/2015/04/all-business-class-flights-return-joe-brancatelli.html. Both accessed December 29, 2015.

question, "Where *is* value being created and destroyed within the transportation ecosystem, and how *do* we capture its new sources of value?"

Answering this question led Etihad to a series of programs focused on doing more with less (cost optimization) and building out new services with greater quality (doing what they were doing better). However, searching to answer this question also led to another set of activities explicitly focused on capturing new sources of value. This required turning the question around—from an inside-out perspective to an outside-in perspective, from the customer's perspective. Doing so led them to ask, "What is an airline for? What does it afford, or enable, folks to do?" Answering these questions might lead to entirely new types of value, and growth possibilities, to deliver.

Airplanes, if you cut through all of their engineering complexity, are vehicles *to do* something. They *afford* the opportunity for people to meet specific objectives to do what they need to do by traveling from point A to point B. If you're looking to catalyze new sources of value within the customer's ecosystem, *from their perspective*, then exploring what an airline affords people to do provides provocative insight into where to play and how to do so.

The shift in focus here is critical. One option that an airline can consider when starting out along a strategic journey is to start with its core assets—planes, seats, and service—and explore how they can do more with them. Another option is to look at the needs from the passengers' perspectives and ask what it is that the airline helps folks do and then orchestrate capabilities, products, and services to help meet those needs. This shift of focus—*from what you have to what your products afford customers to do*—will (a) identify new opportunities of value to capture and (b) require new capabilities to do so.

Some of these new capabilities will go beyond what you have done so well to date. They will require new types of partnerships and/or alliances with different types of firms to provide them. They will need to be orchestrated. They will require new business models to execute.

With this as context, what *is* an airline for? What does it *afford* folks to do, the jobs they want to get done? An airplane, after all, is a vehicle to do something. This something includes—

- Facilitating business and enabling a memorable experience for passengers as they go from one place to another

- Expediently meeting a crisis

  For example, some passengers need to get somewhere to deal with the death or illness of a family or friend. Another example is the use of a plane to support a humanitarian relief effort. A number of airlines allocate a certain number of aircraft, most of which require changes in configuration, which can be mobilized by their host government to support humanitarian relief efforts. The US, for example, has what is called the Civil Reserve Air Fleet (CRAF) program, which signs up US passenger and cargo carriers to make aircraft available at times when the need for airlift exceeds the capability of the military aircraft fleet.

- Deepening infrastructure capabilities

  FedEx is a prime example of an airline which, through its very presence, strengthened a local economy in terms of sustainable jobs created. FedEx ships 3 million packages a day through its Memphis airport and employs more than 30,000 people in the region as of 2015. FedEx didn't start in Memphis but was attracted there by the city's proximity to major Midwest and East Coast markets, as well as a great trucking, rail, and waterway infrastructure. "Memphis has the four r's: runway, road, rail, and river," says Reid Dulberger, the chief economic development officer for Memphis.[58] FedEx has deepened the region's logistics and distribution industry, enabling smooth transfers across the different modes of transportation and building a strong ecosystem of mutually supported businesses to capture the new sources of value.

---

58 John Kasarda and Greg Lindsay, *Aerotropolis: The Way We'll Live Next* (New York: Farrar, Straus and Giroux, 2012). See also: Amanda Kolson Hurley, "The Memphis Airport Is on a Mission to Become Its Own City," Citylab, Aug. 28, 2014, http://www.citylab.com/design/2014/08/the-memphis-airport-is-on-a-mission-to-become-its-own-city/379227/.

- Concentrating specialized expertise

  The logistics expertise required to schedule, maintain, and operate fleets, as airlines do, is profound. It is also fungible in the sense that the deep analytic capabilities underlying it can be used for other transportation areas. There is a knowledge spillover across transportation sectors. What is good and useful for airlines can be good and useful for other modes of transportation like trains, trucks, and ships. Furthermore, specialized knowledge requires specialized training and the infrastructure to support it—e.g., training programs, access to experts, service industries to house the trainers and trainees. In short, this spillover illustrates that specialized expertise leads to job ecosystems with different types of jobs mutually reinforcing each other.

  Specialized capital, or skill, is costly to build, maintain, and grow. And not every business within an ecosystem needs to own it. Some airlines recognized this, which is one reason Delta Airlines made the strategic decision over twenty years ago to build out its maintenance, repair, and overhaul (MRO) skill set and offer it as a service to other airlines. MRO capabilities are cost-buckets rather than sources of differentiation. Consequently, a number of different airlines decided to use Delta's MRO services. This move became a win-win for everyone. Airlines could allocate resources away from MRO, in places they believed they could get a better return on their investment. For Delta, it became an additional revenue source; they monetized what was before merely an expense item (and a large one at that).

Etihad—Lesson #2: Business Model Innovation, to Shift Risks and Increase Returns

Etihad was founded out of Abu Dhabi and designed initially to support travel throughout parts of the Middle East, specifically the Gulf Cooperation Countries (or GCC). A number of their passengers traveled throughout specific countries in Africa as well, which triggered their expansion to include these areas. Africa has a number of different airlines serving local markets, many at extremely low fares relative to the larger airline carriers.

Etihad quickly recognized the opportunity to increase their passenger base by getting access to passengers of these regional airlines. Doing so would give them a foothold into new regions and boost their passenger count while increasing the likelihood that these passengers would be *locked-in* to Etihad when and if they decided to travel elsewhere. Executing on this involved establishing minority positions with a number of the regional airlines, which Etihad did, with Air Seychelles as an early example.[59] The brilliance of this move stemmed from getting access to new passengers but keeping much of the risk of financial performance with the regional airline. Executing on it also required new pricing and marketing programs to attract people who had never, or seldom, flown (note: classic example of nonconsumption and/or market breakdown, sources for explosive growth). Etihad's partnership strategy has been one of serving what are called *third-tier locations*, those that are typically perceived to be too low cost to make it profitable for the larger carriers to service. Etihad's innovative business model of designing a network of partnerships has proven this perception to be false.

Value seen is value captured. James recognized this, saw the opportunity in minimal or nonconsumption, and designed a set of interwoven relationships among carriers and other services, including airport, logistics, and hospitality businesses, to capture to great effect this previously ignored source of value.

Three Lessons Beyond Customer Centricity to Ecosystems of Engagement

Explosive growth is the game to play. Incremental growth is based on doing more of the same, only better. Customer centricity, for all the reasons already discussed, is critical in order to remain and sustain ongoing

---

59   Ivo Pezelj, "Differentiation in Strategy Is Key to Etihad Airways' Success," Aug. 7, 2013, http://www. aspireaviation.com/2013/08/07/etihad-airways-equity-alliance-strategy/. See also "Airlines 2020: Substitution and Commoditization," IBM Institute for Business Value, Dec. 2010, http://www-935.ibm.com/services/ multimedia/uk_en_airlines_2020.pdf. Both accessed December 29, 2015.

relevance—hence its siren call that nearly every firm in every part of the world in every industry is following.

However, returning to the first question that teed up this chapter, if everyone is running down this path, what (other than running the outexecute race) will be distinctive, (importantly) sustainable, and (critically) explosive?

The key to the explosive growth of some of the companies we mentioned, and that leaders of tomorrow will follow, is a pragmatic set of steps:

1. Understand the ecosystem in which your customer engages.
2. Mobilize around the new foundations of value that underlie *that* ecosystem.
3. Shape the experience in it.
4. Control the core sources of value that drive it to shape its downstream allocation.
5. Orchestrate the capabilities from other actors to do so.

Got it.

But there are three additional takeaways—specific insights—to help you take advantage of the steps outlined above.

First: Take Advantage of Insights That Customer Affordance "Affords"

In short, the concept of affordances—

- Points to new potential sources of value, in the ecosystems in which customers spend their time, money, and effort

- Prioritizes what the new 20 percent of capabilities (and hence new products/services) are needed to capture that value

- Helps to frame out new business models to execute

Recall: The customer affordance map helps identify new capabilities and potential actors to engage to orchestrate and thereby capture new sources of value *from the customer's perspective*. For example, each of the airline affordances requires (a) new capabilities to capitalize on them; (b) new partnerships with other organizations—many outside the transportation realm—which bring differing capabilities to the table; and (c) new business models to execute on both. The point here is broader, with Etihad being only an example to highlight the same lesson, whether you are Etihad or Converse, Nike or Schneider, Chamberlain or Unifrax, the Veteran's Administration or Aetna, Facebook or Samsung, Merck or Novartis, etc. The concept of affordances complements the traditional approach to customer segmentation and customer journey maps. It provides a tangible technique to explore and highlight the opportunities of potential new sources of value from your customer's perspective and the orchestration of capabilities from a wide range of firms needed to capture that value.

Let's consider Eamonn Kelly's observation: People don't want physicians, hospitals, and pharmaceuticals; they want wellness.[60] Or Dan Wollenberg's: People don't want checking or savings accounts; they want financial security. Or Jared's of Converse: People don't want more sneakers; they want expressions of their individual style. Each of these needs will not, and cannot, be met by SIC-confined businesses; they require the orchestration of different capabilities, delivered by a broad range of organizations—hence the pragmatic steps to take to go beyond traditional approaches to customer centricity, with implications for where to focus, how to do so, and with whom to engage to execute.

Second: Recognize That There Exist Three Different Types (Generations) of Customer Journey Maps, and It Matters Which One You Use

Companies that grow (effectively) are those that capture customers' attention.

Scale and explosive growth used to come from ownership of supply; think telecommunications with its wires, Comcast and its network, automobile companies and their supply chains, utilities and their infrastructure.

---

60   Discussion with Gail Cassell, former president of American Society of Microbiology and chairwoman of multiple IoM (Institute of Medicine) commissions and reports, Dec. 2016.

But scale and growth don't come from those sources anymore. The rise of the Internet and the capability to acquire customers at a near-zero marginal cost has shifted scale and growth to the demand side of the equation—namely, to those who know how to interact with customers effectively, through orchestrating capabilities from the supply side but delivering through new and different types of distribution channels. The competitive game comes down, as we've all heard loudly and clearly, to customer experience—but a different perspective on customer experience, and centricity, as we've pointed out throughout this section.

Customer experience is typically reduced to the ease of interaction with one's products and services. This has led to much money and effort spent on customer journey mapping to identify the "pain points" from a customer's perspective regarding how they use your product or service. Two of the three generations of customer journey mapping fall into this camp.

Generation 1 involves the mapping of one's product to where, when, and how a customer engages with it to identify points of friction that could be eliminated. Its objective: make the process simpler (and faster) to engage with.

Generation 2 is similar but adds an emotional element to it. It also consists of a map of a product process to where, when, and how a customer engages within that journey. It adds, however, another layer to the mapping that focuses on points of emotional tension or "sources of happiness." Its objective: understand the pivot points of emotional engagement across a process to make the process simpler (and faster) to engage with.

Both of these are fine approaches. However, they remain tied to engaging with a set of products and/or services you already have. Their starting point: "You have a problem to fix with respect to how customers engage with your existing set of products and services." Both are fine for supporting incremental growth or productivity enhancements, which is why they are so prevalent and important to do.

However, taking lessons from today's growth leaders, we find that customer experience is based on the orchestration of capabilities and services to help customers *get done what they want or need to get done* in an ecosystem of friction to tackle or nonconsumption to overcome, with different organizations, capabilities, and bundles of products and services. Enter the new third generation of customer journey insight.

Generation 3 starts with an outside-in perspective, independent of the products and services (and underlying processes) you provide. The questions underlying this third generation become, What is it that customers want to do, and what are the ecosystems in which they spend their time, monies, and efforts to do it? How do you engage in *those*?

What you use depends on what your objectives are.

Third: Affordance Is More Than Doing Things Differently; It's Also about Becoming Someone Different

The customer affordance framework is a powerful and pragmatic one. It is key to answering the new strategic question of where value is being created—and destroyed—in the ecosystems in which our customers engage. Like a prism, it sheds three different types of light onto those ecosystems: one, on where to focus and what to do within that new focus; two, on how to engage your customers differently; three, on who you are and the core role/identity that creates a new relationship with your customers and their ecosystem.

Let's think about this.

Explosive growth comes from transforming what was previously unknown, considered too hard to do, or just plain ignored into new sources of value, powered by new capabilities, products, and services delivered in new ways. Transformation, a fancy word, simply reflects a change in logic of how something was done before catalyzing new value to capture in new ways. It reminds us of a cult movie, *The Gods Must Be Crazy*. In it, a character in the Kalahari Desert finds a Coke bottle, something never before seen by him or his tribe. It becomes heralded as a disruptive object with supernatural powers, catalyzing (in the movie) a hilarious set of new relationships and activities. The relevant quote from the movie is, "Things that were yesterday unknown have today become a necessity."

That's what transformation does: It catalyzes new ways to make sense and take action around topics, challenges, and opportunities that yesterday were unknown, today are becoming distinctive, and tomorrow will become regular (and expected) methods of engagement.

So it is with tackling market friction and nonconsumption, planting a flag around them, and mobilizing new capabilities both to "own" and to create explosive growth as a result.

But funny things happen as you go down a transformation pathway. Of course, you need new capabilities to support it. And of course you need a new business model to execute with speed and scale. But transformation is not only what it is you do and how you do it; it is also about changes in behavior, expectation, and yes, identity of consumers as well. And here it gets extremely interesting—and begins to point out a new window into explosive growth for those who choose to open it.

Let's first look at a quick example of what we're talking about and then close out this section with specific considerations.

Facebook once famously said that "we want to be the dial tone for the Internet." Earlier, we explored this statement in the context of how to start making sense of ecosystem economics. Here we'll explore it from a different perspective, from where explosive value comes from.

Let's start by extending a commonly asked question from "how do we improve our products/services in ways our customers want us to" to "what is it that our products/services afford our customers to do?"

Facebook's focus on becoming the dial tone has had profound affordance implications. It has done much more than simply impact what customers do; it has changed who they are and how they engage with each other to *become* someone different. No, this is not too broad of a claim. Think about it.

Facebook asked its users to become more open and to share their personal information. Millennials jumped all over this and now seem unfazed by sharing an enormous amount of information that many of those who went before them—e.g., their parents, bosses, teachers—once considered private and no one else's business. This has striking implications—from a staggering amount of information that one can gather about people, certainly any with a digital footprint, to extensive and profound policy and professional discussions of what counts as private, personal, confidential information, as well as how to share, protect, and yes, even monetize that information. Facebook nudged us to become someone different. And we responded.

But it's not just Facebook that has afforded such behavioral change not only in what we do and how we do it but also in who we become while doing so. As Tim O'Reilly reminds us, "Amazon turned shoppers into information-rich consumers who could share real-time data and reviews, cross-check prices, and weigh algorithmic recommendations on their path to online purchase. Who shops now without doing at least some digital comparisons of price and performance? Successful innovators ask users to embrace—or at least tolerate—new values, new skills, new behaviors, new vocabulary, new ideas, new expectations, and new aspirations. *They transform their customers.*" [61] He cites Michael Schrage, a commentator on innovation from MIT, on a more contemporary example: "When Apple television advertisements show iPhone users asking Siri questions or telling 'her' what to do, the company is doing far more than showing off the versatility of its voice-recognition artificial intelligence interface. Siri's company asks its customers to become the sort of people who wouldn't think twice about talking to their phone as a sentient servant." [62]

Recall that business model innovation, powered by business ecosystems, is all about identifying and capturing new sources of value in new ways. What worked before no longer will. This has been one of the main recurring drumbeats throughout the book. Recall that as organizations have gone down this path, they have had to reexamine (a) what

---

61 Tim O'Reilly, "We Got This Whole Unicorn Thing Wrong," Medium.com, accessed January 23, 2016, https://medium.com/the-wtf-economy/we-ve-got-this-whole-unicorn-thing-all-wrong-3f3d108cc71d#.orzvmm2xw. Italics added.

62 Ibid. Also see Sherry Turkle, *Reclaiming Conversation: The Power of Talk in a Digital Age* (New York: Penguin Press, 2015).

their new foundations of value would be (i.e., where to focus); (b) how they were going to orchestrate capabilities to do so (i.e., business model innovation); and (c) what that meant in terms of how they showed up to their customers, their markets, and their stakeholders (i.e., their identity). As examples, merely recall some of our discussion around Dylan at Metropolitan Health, a Moss Adams COO, Cisco's shift, MoDe's position, Etihad's transformation, and of course the typical FANG players of Facebook, Amazon, Netflix, and Google (to name but a few).

Section Summary: Where Does This Take Us, and Now What?

Yes, the new game is around the quality of experience and the capability to scale—with customers as the new control point to create and allocate value. The *what* to do isn't in doubt. It's the *how* to do it that, for most, remains challenging—and what this book seeks to overcome.

From the Experience Economy to Transformational Engagement

Our new competitive landscape requires business model innovation, powered by business ecosystems around explosive new growth opportunities. The way to make this happen is to plant a flag around critical problems—specific customer or market needs, friction, and areas of non-consumption—and mobilize new capabilities in new ways both to "own" and to execute around that flag. Asking and answering the new strategic questions are the ways to determine where to play, how to focus, and how to execute.

With this in mind, it's interesting to return to what has led us to our changing competitive landscape.

At the turn of the century, only a short while ago, we started moving from the so-called Information Age, powered by the rise of the Internet and much greater technology connectivity capabilities, to what the futurist Alvin

Toffler called the Experience Economy. This period has seen an explosion in customer centricity, in work on emotional intelligence and sensitivity to strengthening the culture of engagement. As the authors Steven Kotler and Jamie Wheal point out, "This is why retail shops started to look like theme parks. Why, instead of stocking ammo on their shelves like Wal-Mart, the outdoor retailer Cabela's turns their stores into a hunter's paradise of big-game mounts, faux mountainsides, and giant aquariums. It's how Starbucks can charge four dollars for a fifty-cent cup of coffee: because they're providing that cozy 'third place' between work and home."[63]

We're now shifting again, from an experience economy to a transformational one. Simply look at some of today's explosive-growth companies and what they promise. We've already discussed Facebook and the transformation it catalyzed both of what we do and who we are. But look also at companies like CrossFit or Soul Cycle with a similar promise to transform you—in terms of what you look like if you engage within a community powered by their rituals and capabilities. Their commitment is not merely that you'll look more fit but, because of the challenging routines and pushing boundaries they put you through, you will begin to act and think differently as well. Back to Kotler and Wheal, "That's a positive 'transformation' that many are willing to suffer and pay a premium for."[64]

Here's the point. Transformation requires a big bet around where to focus and how to execute to capture explosive sources of value. It is not about doing incrementally better but about catalyzing something dramatically and radically different. Explosive growth will always come from such differences—from insight into new areas of focus (around customer needs from their perspective, market friction, and/or nonconsumption) and new business models, powered by business ecosystems to execute on them. This is why the imperative is to go beyond our traditional conceptions of customer experience to the ecosystems in which that experience can be dramatically enhanced and engaged. Otherwise, why bother?

---

63 Steven Kotler and Jamie Wheal, *Stealing Fire: How Silicon Valley, the Navy SEALs, and Maverick Scientists are Revolutionizing the Way We Live and Work* (New York: Day Street, 2017): 195.

64 Ibid.

From Insight to Action

Reading books is one thing. Knowing how to apply their insights is often quite another. The fundamental premise of this book is simple, though its implications are, we believe, important.

The Pragmatics of Execution

Historically, technological advances have always outstripped our capability to figure out what to do with them. Who knew the extraordinary ramifications of splitting the atom? The development of the transistor? Who can foresee for sure the implications of extended reality—the combination of augmented reality with virtual reality? Of machine learning? These ramifications were and will be observed, understood, and, over time, harnessed through the development of new business models able to direct them toward both social and economic ends. Yet it takes time to figure out how to do this. In short, technological advances always create two types of gaps that need to be filled:

- Gap #1: between technology advances and figuring out their implications and what to do with them

- Gap #2: between figuring out what to do with them and how to take advantage of the opportunities they create

Today we are frequently reminded that both of these gaps are merely getting wider, faster. Machine learning, cognitive insight, and what some call the Age of Algorithms are additional proof points of accelerating technological advances, making closing the gaps harder—and some say, impossible.

Wrestling through the answers to the new strategic questions helps you close these two gaps. Our competitive landscape has changed, driven by shifts in technology and in economic and social logics, as we've discussed. We use the word *logics* for a specific reason. Logic is no more than a set of internally consistent rules that guide behavior. Those rules rest on a shared assumption that triggers the rules to follow. Change the assumption, and the rules or logic you follow no longer work.

Today's new market leaders recognize that a changed world requires new strategic questions. This new strategic question requires taking a new unit of focus—that of the ecosystem in which you, and your customers, are engaged. As a friend of ours likes to say, "The *challenge* is how to identify and capture new sources of value in new ways. And the *opportunity* is . . . how to identify and capture new sources of value in new ways." Asking the new strategic questions is the first step to getting started. The second step, and objective of this book, is to help you start answering them. We have used many examples throughout the book, drawn from different industries and different geographies, to help you take these two steps.

Section Road Map

This final section consists of two chapters.

Chapter 7 is a field guide for steps to take. It pulls together (briefly) the models and frameworks used as well as the lessons suggested in an easy-to-(re)use manner. It also shows how they can be and have been used to support new strategic journeys to identify and capture new sources of explosive value.

Chapter 8 concludes with a reflection on key insights and how new business models, powered by ecosystem-centric strategies, can be pointed to tackle ever broader, harder "wicked problems" to create both greater economic value and societal impact.

7

Field Guide for the
New Strategic Questions

Examples serve a pragmatic purpose: to provide color commentary on the topic discussed. Those that resonate have a secondary purpose: to suggest how specific examples might be of potential use. These examples highlight new ways to think about old challenges. These new ways are reflected in models. Models are merely mechanisms, or tools, to help us visualize or think about challenges differently. Each model provides insight into some aspect of business ecosystems. Together, they form a tapestry of insight to help us identify and capture new sources of value in new ways.

The Use of Examples—as Keys to Make Sense of Business Ecosystems and What You Can Do about Them

Many people have asked us to show how different types of business ecosystems, models, and insights fit together. This chapter was added in response to their request that we add a *field guide* or toolkit section on how to use some of the models to help them answer the new strategic questions. To that end, this chapter is divided into two major sections:

- Section 1 briefly describes each model in terms of what it does, what part of the strategic questions it answers, and how it can be used.

- Section 2 briefly describes how a number of these models and their insights fit together, using three specific examples based on actual projects.

These projects each have a different objective. But they are all based on how to capture new sources of value from an ecosystem perspective. We selected these projects for three pragmatic reasons. First, they focus on different—but common—types of questions many organizations attempt to answer. Second, they reflect different sponsors within an organization. And third, they reflect different time frames of execution. The three different types of examples are—

- Digital transformation—with the core objective to identify and catalyze new sources of value in new ways

- New consumer engagement model—with the core objective to design a new consumer engagement model around new sources of value

- Optimizing an innovation and R&D portfolio—with the core objective to increase the likelihood of "hitting it big" (to quote the sponsor, the CEO) on their big-bet portfolio

What's common to each of these journeys is more important than what separates them. First, they all strive to get insight into where value is being created and destroyed in the ecosystems in which they are engaged. Second, they are examples of how the models can be used to drive that insight. Together these two sections are intended to provide pragmatic examples for you to begin using their insights to support your own journeys.

Methods and Models to Answer the Strategic Questions

The following table lists and briefly describes each model according to the different type of insight it provides. The rest of this section describes each model's focus and explains why it is important and how it is used.

What they are	What they provide	How they're useful
Ecosystem Models		
Ecosystem Maps	Clarity about what makes up the ecosystem: who is involved, the roles they perform, and how they interact	Depicts who/what makes up the ecosystem you and your customers are engaged in and establishes a baseline of where you play today—and may tomorrow
Ecosystem Types	A framework to clarify and distinguish among different types of ecosystem-centric business models that exist	Serves as a diagnostic regarding which types—or patterns—may be relevant to you given your objectives, the role you might play within them, and the capabilities critical to doing so
Ecosystem Friction Table	Insight into the essential roles, sources of value, capabilities, and challenges each stakeholder plays within your ecosystem so you can figure out how to engage them	Isolates the new 20 percent of critical capabilities—as well as helps identify potential new types of players who will be part of your new ecosystem to engage
Ecosystem Value Distribution	Insight into where value is shifting within your ecosystem	Provides insight into shifting profit and growth pools and thereby input into potential new areas to focus on
Total Ecosystem Opportunity (TEO)	Insight into the total economic opportunity around specific market needs from an ecosystem perspective	Reframes where to focus in terms of new profit and/or growth pools, from a market needs—rather than industry—perspective
Consumer Engagement Models		
Touchpoint Triangle	Depiction and diagnostic framework of a pragmatic balance among products, services, and experience capabilities	Focuses discussion around what products, services, and experiences mean and entail, given shifting expectations and capabilities needed to support them all
Consumer Ecosystem Engagement Model	Insights into the ecosystems that your customers care about—in terms of where they spend their time, energy, and resources	Refocuses attention toward new sources of value, from the customer's perspective, not with respect to the usability of your products or services but from their usefulness, outcomes, or jobs-to-be-done perspective

What they are	What they provide	How they're useful
Value Insight Models		
Bundle/Unbundle Framework	Insight into shifting economics from a value chain perspective	Focuses attention on new sources of economic value, with implications for changes to your business model and the new critical capabilities needed
New Foundations/Value Vectors	Visual depiction of the essential foundations of value that underlie industry transformation and customer needs—arguably, one of the most critical models	Simplifies and clarifies the essential sources of value to focus on—of what to do, when, and how to do so
Currency Maps	Insight to identify and assess different types of value that matter to and mobilize different types of stakeholders	Enables different perspectives to have an equal voice when wrestling through investment choices of who to focus on to do what
Value Influence Diagram	Insight into different sets of activities that drive different types of value and the interaction among them to do so	Isolates key levers to push to accelerate impact—through making clear the dependencies of activities on each other
Asset Rate Curve	Insight into the rate at which key capabilities, or assets, decrease or increase their value over time—a simple visualization to get executives to step above their day-to-day activities to reevaluate the core assets that drive value for their business	Provides a framework to align around, discuss, and prioritize your core capabilities
The New 20 Percent Models		
The New 20 Percent	Depiction of the new capabilities (assets, skill sets, competencies) critical to capturing 70 percent of the new sources of value	Focuses attention on the new capabilities that you need to capture new sources of value and thereby provide input into both a development and migration plan for existing and new capabilities
Business Ecosystem Canvas	Snapshot into core elements that make up the specific type of business ecosystem as well as your role within it	Extends a commonly used framework to communicate business focus—here, from an ecosystem perspective
Reference Architectures	Visual depiction of business and technology capabilities	Clarifies what folks are talking about and the implications different projects will have for different parts of the business; also clarifies who within one's ecosystem performs what set of activities

Ecosystem Models

What follows is a description of each of the above listed models: what they are, why they're useful, and how to use them. Not all of them will be used or even useful for every strategic journey. Think of these as a set of tools that make up your new strategic toolkit. Like any great carpenter, you bring the tools you need for the job at hand—no more, no less. It's figuring out which ones to use when that will become a critical new capability, taking you from strategic intent to pragmatic execution. The following section is a start toward strengthening that capability.

Ecosystem Map

What It Is

Visual representations of relationships among different types of organizations. It shows how they interact with each other and the types of activities that tie them together. This is done from two perspectives:

- Actor-based: this map focuses on specific organizations that make up your ecosystem
- Role-based: this map is capability-based rather than industry or SIC code–based.

The results include a heat map of the current state of the ecosystem and where value is being created and destroyed today within it.

What It Provides

Clarity of what makes up the ecosystem in terms of who is involved, the roles they perform, and how they interact.

Why It Matters

It takes a village to capture new sources of value. Clarifying what makes an ecosystem—including the types of stakeholders, roles, and capabilities that catalyze and hold it together—helps identify new opportunities that ecosystems enable.

These models serve as a baseline for understanding today's competitive landscape and those of tomorrow. They are used both at the start as well as throughout a process as your team's understanding of its ecosystem gets richer and the implications for what you might do get clearer. They provide—

- Insight into actors relevant to specific friction or market need, those with both direct and indirect impact
- Perspective on new types of actors relevant to capturing new sources of value
- Insight into potential areas of engagement
- Perspective on potential actors or roles to engage in different ways
- A new language to talk about where and how to capture new sources of value within your ecosystem

Questions It Helps Answer

What is our ecosystem? What types of actors and stakeholders make it up? What roles do they perform within it? What activities—and different types of value—hold it together? How do we anticipate and understand the implications of the ripple effects of decisions made and actions taken by different stakeholders within it? Which ones are important today and critical tomorrow? How do we start to think about how to mobilize different types of stakeholders with different interests and motivations in a way that increases value to everyone? Different types of ecosystem models exist. Which one(s) are relevant for us, and what role might we play within them?

Ecosystem Types
What It Is
Visual depictions of different types of business ecosystems that exist. This depiction takes the form of a spider chart, allowing visual comparison

across different types of possible business ecosystems and consequently ones more or less relevant, given your objective and/or the type of value to capture. These models are complementary to the Ecosystem Business Canvas (description follows).

What It Provides

A framework to clarify and distinguish among different types of ecosystem-centric business models that exist.

Why It Matters

Different types of business ecosystems exist. Insight into these different types helps to identify—

- Which ones might be relevant, given your objectives
- What roles you might play within them
- The types of capabilities needed to do so

Questions It Helps Answer

What different business ecosystems might be relevant for what we want to do? What role might we play within them? What capabilities are critical to doing so? What are the different types of actors that make up the relevant business model?

Ecosystem Friction Table

What It Is

A table mapping stakeholders to a number of different attributes, each of which sheds light into different methods for engaging different types of stakeholders.

What It Provides

Insight into the essential roles, sources of value, capabilities, and challenges—e.g., frictions or breakdowns—each stakeholder faces. This information helps you begin to figure out how to engage them and what capabilities are needed to do so.

Why It Matters

Different types of actors within your ecosystem are motivated differently. What *matters* to them—or, stated differently, what constitutes value—differs. Nonprofits, for example, need money to run their operations; however, they are purpose- or mission-driven organizations motivated by their mission, whatever it is, and measure themselves accordingly. Even within a typical for-profit organization, executives who perform different roles are motivated—or incentivized—by different types of value. Those who focus on energy sustainability, for example, see their world through the lens of impact on carbon footprint or other measures of sustainability; the head of human resources, the quality of talent they bring into the firm; academic hospitals, at least the majority of physicians within them, are motivated by health outcomes rather than department profitability; and so on. Insight into what motivates different types of actors within your ecosystem is critical to helping you figure out how to engage them. In short, the breakdown table matters because it—

- Clarifies what types of value matters to different stakeholders
- Suggests how to motivate different types of stakeholders

Questions It Helps Answer

What role does each stakeholder play within the ecosystem? After all, an ecosystem is the orchestration of capabilities across different types of actors in a complementary way to provide value for all of them. Other key questions include, What key capabilities does each stakeholder bring to the table? What challenges—or frictions—does each stakeholder face to realize the value they care about? What capabilities are needed to overcome those frictions? Who—i.e., what types of stakeholders or roles—provide those capabilities? How might insight into these friction points suggest where you might focus or the capabilities you would need—either to engage these stakeholders (differently) or to capture new sources of value?

Ecosystem—Value Distribution

What It Is

A graphical depiction of where value is allocated across the ecosystem. We have built dynamic ones, based on Monte Carlo simulations that allow you to play *what if* games based on the placement of graphical slid- ers. Output from the simulations converts into rich visualizations that dynamically shift the representations we depict below.

What It Provides

Insight into where value is shifting within your ecosystem.

Why It Matters

It is one thing to map out an ecosystem. It is another to figure out how value is distributed within it today and then tomorrow. Insight into today's distribution and how that may shift tomorrow helps to focus attention on potential new sources of growth.

In short, the value distribution charts matter because they—

- Expose dependencies among critical activities—*levers to pull*, as one of our clients called it—to accelerate or slow down value realization

- Help to challenge—or *stress-test,* as another called it—programs to ensure that the right levers are being pulled.

Questions It Helps Answer

How—and where—is value shifting within the ecosystem in which you are engaged? This model, combined with some of the others, such as sim- ulation work, provides a rigorous method of sensitivity analysis regarding decisions made and actions taken. Playing *what if* games regarding how value could and is likely to shift, depending on one's role within an ecosystem, is helpful input into strategic planning.

Ecosystem—Total Ecosystem Opportunity (TEO)
What It Is
A framework to evaluate the total economic opportunity from an ecosystem perspective.

What It Provides
Insight into the total economic opportunity around specific market needs from an ecosystem perspective. Specifically, it provides insight into—

- Economic opportunities around a specific set of customer needs— perhaps previously unseen and hence uncaptured
- Possible winners and losers as the shape of ecosystems changes
- Potential methods to capture that value

Why It Matters
Typical approaches to identifying one's market opportunity include looking at the potential spend of consumers within an industry around a specific set of products or services. Companies typically define their total addressable market (known as TAM) consisting of folks who do or might want to purchase their products. The TAM is typically calculated by taking this set of folks—segmented by age, geography, and so on—and multiplying it by an estimated spend on products. This estimated spend is typically some derivative of estimated GDP growth, consumer confidence, discretionary income, and other considerations.

TAM is a fine exercise to go through. It's just too limiting from an ecosystem perspective, missing the new opportunities that the perspective opens up.

Instead, we believe it's important to identify where and how to capture value within your ecosystem. Answering *this* question requires insight into the total economic opportunity (TEO) and value of your ecosystem.

Why does TEO matter?

- It estimates the total ecosystem opportunity (TEO) that exists around a new source of value.

- It helps to isolate what parts of that TEO may be relevant for an organization to focus on.

- It helps to identify potential partnerships to capture other parts of the TEO.

Questions It Helps Answer

What is the total ecosystem opportunity around new sources of value? What part of that TEO might we focus on? Of that focus, what new capabilities would be needed to capture it?

Consumer Engagement Models

It is no longer enough to provide the desired product, service, or experience. The *job to be done* in Clayton Christensen's formulation is merely the beginning. Planting a flag on specific sets of customer needs and the orchestration of capabilities required to meet them requires a change in an organization's focus from both that of the firm or a particular customer to the ecosystem in which *they both engage*. It's not enough to talk about customer centricity or the customer journey. It is important to look at the ecosystem *from the customer's perspective* and change the unit of focus. This entails understanding the ecosystems in which they engage:

- The combination of products, services, and experiences that support that engagement

- Where, why, and how they spend their energy, time, and resources

- The outcomes and expectations that matter to them

Only this understanding will clarify what the customer's friction or needs are to overcome and the capabilities critical to meeting them. Then, and only then, will you be able to see the universe of possibilities to orchestrate those capabilities to capture new sources of value in new ways.

Questions to Ask and Answer

What are the ecosystems in which our customers engage? And what are the specific sources of needs, as threaded through the lenses of market friction, breakdown, and/or nonconsumption that our existing and potential customers care about? What are the capabilities needed to meet those needs from their perspective?

The Touchpoint Triangle
What It Is
A simple graphic that depicts—

- A balance among products, services, and experience-based capabilities to engage your customers in new ways
- The changing of this balance over time

What It Provides
A depiction of a balance among products, services, and experience capabilities and a framework to evaluate how you engage your customers (focusing on outcomes and expectations—the new customer touchpoints).

Why It Matters
What product company is not looking to build services to complement what it does? What service company is not exploring how to productize their services? What do services even mean for a product company? What capabilities are needed to support them? How different are these

capabilities from the ones needed to support their core business? And what are the implications for the people, the revenue, and the business model in making these shifts? The same questions are relevant for product companies and their exploration into services. And what companies are not looking to improve their customer experience? These are critical questions. Yet many companies wrestle with how to even have these conversations, much less execute on them. The Touchpoint Triangle is a simple starting point to trigger this discussion. It matters because it—

- Visualizes the balance among products, services, and experiences over time

- Provides a simple way to explore this balance

- Begins to wrestle through the implications of what a changing mix among products, services, and experiences could mean over time in terms of capabilities, migration plans, investments, and customer engagement

Questions It Helps Answer

What is the balance among products, services, and experiences to capture new sources of value? What is your balance today? Tomorrow? What are the effects of this changing balance on what you do today, tomorrow?

Customer Ecosystem Engagement Model

What It Is

Visual depiction of the ecosystems consumers care about and consequently roles you might consider for capturing new sources of value within these ecosystems.

What It Provides

Insights into the ecosystems that your customers care about in terms of where they spend their time, energy, and resources.

Why It Matters

Customer ecosystem engagement models help you—

- Visualize the overlapping ecosystems that customers care about in terms of where they spend their time, energy, and resources (from this perspective, it complements and abstracts customer segmentation studies)
- Distill critical capabilities needed for engaging within these ecosystems
- Point to different types of organizations critical to these consumer ecosystems
- Identify possible new partners you may work with and roles that you might perform within these ecosystems

Questions It Helps Answer

Where are customers spending their time, energy, and resources? What are the implications of their focus in terms of how value is shifting across our value chains and within our ecosystem? What are the implications for new capabilities we might want to consider and roles to perform to capture this focus? And finally, what other stakeholders might we need to engage to do so?

Value Insight Models

Explosive growth and value creation has historically come from tackling friction, market breakdown, and/or nonconsumption.[65] It is no different now. Consequently, we need fast, pragmatic ways to identify these needs and untapped sources of value. Orchestrating capabilities from different types of organizations to capture the resulting potential value is essential. The following models provide insights into potential areas for disruption

---

65   Eric Beinhocker, *The Origin of Wealth: The Radical Remaking of Economics and What It Means for Business and Society* (Boston: Harvard Business Review Press, 2007).

(untapped opportunities), as well as the creation of new value not captured by established players.

Questions to Ask, and Answer, of This Set of Models

Where is value being created and destroyed in our ecosystem? How is value being distributed across various players within the ecosystem? Who are the (potential) new winners and losers, with the implications of where we might focus, folks we might partner with, and capabilities to do so?

Bundle/Unbundle Framework

What It Is

A graphic depiction of value chains that highlights—

- The relative contribution to revenue and profit
- The changing dynamic of those contributions
- The likely industry (or cross-industry) aggregation (bundling) or disaggregation (unbundling) to capture those changes in revenue and profit contribution

What It Provides

Insights into how value is distributed across value chains within an ecosystem. It suggests both where and why the value chains are being aggregated (bundled) or disaggregated (unbundled).

Why It Matters

Industry lines are blurring. Technological advances, regulatory shifts, and customer expectations impact every industry. Patterns exist in terms of what these impacts are. The bundle/unbundle models are one way to identify what some of these patterns are. This identification helps to assess what's going on within any one industry and across industries.

In short, the bundle/unbundle models matter because they provide quick visual insights into—

- Changing economics of an industry, from a value chain perspective
- Potential areas to focus on, across industry borders, depending on the specific new sources of value you are exploring
- Potential new actors to engage to capture either the newly bundled or unbundled parts of a value chain
- Patterns of blurring across industries, which provide insight into what's common or unique within specific industries

These models provide a snapshot into where your industry is being disaggregated (unbundled) and, in many industries, is being rebundled around new sources of value, from a value chain perspective. Overlaying your understanding of customer needs from the Customer Engagement Model enables you to identify white space opportunities in the ecosystem—places where customer needs are unmet or are likely to increase significantly.

Questions It Helps Answer

How is value shifting across your value chains? What are some of the implications of these shifts regarding new capabilities, of where you are—or are likely to face—margin pressures? What are implications of these shifts on your existing and potentially new sets of customers in terms of what they need or want? Where are likely new pools of profit and growth to explore? And what are the implications of moving toward these shifts?

Note

Initially a number of our clients expressed wariness that these bundle/unbundle models could be useful. Their concern came from the perspective that their industry was unique enough to make comparisons across industries challenging and insufficiently insightful. Their concerns were all put aside. Every industry faces similar challenges; the very activities that are facing each of them require common responses from all of them.

From this perspective, it is not only possible but also helpful to abstract value chains across industries. It is this very abstraction that makes it helpful to see the patterns that underlie blurring across industries and opportunities to capture new sources of value within them.

New Foundations of Value/Value Vectors
What It Is
A visualization that depicts the essential foundations of value to capture. Part of this visualization includes what are known as *linked diagrams* of the sets of capabilities critical to capturing more of this value over time.

What It Provides

Insight and focus around the new foundations of value, and differentiation, that underlie industry transformation.

Why It Matters

As we discussed in Chapter 2, ecosystems are orchestrated around essential types of value to deliver—with *essential* being the key word, pointing to the essence of value that underlies industry transformation around new customer needs.

Nearly thirty years ago, Treacy and Wiersema wrote *The Discipline of Market Leaders*, depicting pragmatic choices for organizations to compete or deliver value effectively.[66] Organizations, they argued, could compete on efficiency (being the low-cost provider), customer intimacy (delivering exceptional customer insight or experience), or innovation (being the new product developer/early adopter). Organizations could and should compete on any two of these three vectors. Attempting to compete on all three made no sense, due to resource constraints and risks of diffusing executional focus. Clearly lots of activities and investments made up each of these vectors.

---

66   Michael Treacy and Fred Wiersema, *The Discipline of Market Leaders* (New York: Basic Books, 1997).

Yet having a simple way to visually depict the value disciplines was helpful for organizations to wrestle through what their *value stance* ought to be, to use the author's words. Clarify your value stance and you have a pragmatic way to figure out how to prioritize what to do, with whom, and when. It's a provocative book, providing a simple framework to motivate discussion. For years we have modified their framework for an ecosystem perspective. The Value Vector extends it to the essential foundations underlying different ecosystems that reflect industry transformation around needs that customers care about.

This framework matters because it—

- Distills the essential sources—or foundations—of value and consequently the value propositions around which to focus efforts and investments

- Provides a simple visual to wrestle through what value one wants to *own*, what role to play, and when to do so

Questions It Helps Answer

What are the new sources of value that underlie our industry? What types of value do you want to capture, and when? What are the critical capabilities and projects needed to do so? When do we focus on deciding on which capabilities to build and programs to execute over time?

Currency Map
What It Is

A currency is a unit of value that motivates the behavior of different stakeholders. Different stakeholders care about—or are motivated by—different types of value, or in our language, currencies. A currency map is the visual depiction of the values that motivate the behavior of different stakeholders and what they care about. It is, from this perspective, a visualization of a shared value framework.

What It Provides

Insights to identify and assess different types of value that matter to and mobilize different types of stakeholders.

Why It Matters

Different types of organizations are motivated by different types of value. Not all of them are motivated by financial return. Carbon footprint, sustainability, brand equity, and societal outcomes are other types of value that motivate their behavior. Currency maps provide visualizations of different types of value that motivate stakeholders. They help to provide a common language to clarify these motivations as well as suggest how to potentially align them to drive collective action. Such insight is critical to figuring out how to influence/shape different types of business ecosystems. These models matter because they—

- Provide a rigorous way to clarify different types of value that matter to different types of stakeholders
- Provide an *equivalency* regarding different types of value important to driving alignment around investment decisions
- Provide input into the creation of any effective shared value framework
- Suggest how to motivate the behavior of different types of stakeholders toward common objectives

Questions It Helps Answer

What motivates different types of actors to do what they do? How can we use that insight to orchestrate different types of actors toward a common objective? How do these currencies change given different decisions made and actions taken? How can we use that insight to figure out when to engage different types of actors at different times?

Value Influence Diagram

What It Is

A systems dynamic model depicting the relationships between key activities and types of value an organization wants to realize. Similar to some of the other items we've described, this model takes the form of static influence diagrams and dynamic ones based on simulations.

What It Provides

Insight into different sets of activities that drive different types of value and the interaction among them to do so.

Why It Matters

The dozens, hundreds, or thousands of activities that organizations perform have ripple effects both within and beyond any one part of an organization. Decisions made and actions taken throughout an organization have both direct and indirect, intended and unintended consequences on the different types of value created. What marketing does impacts everyone in production, customer service, R&D, and beyond to greater and lesser degrees. This diagram is helpful to—

- Identify the essential linkages among activities and the value created (or destroyed)
- Model the ripple effects that impact different types of value
- Isolate critical dependencies of that value creation
- Stress-test that decisions made are having the type of impact desired

Questions It Helps Answer

What are the key activities that drive the type of value we want to create? What are the dependencies among these activities? What are the implications of changing some of these activities—e.g., can we get more or less of this value if we change certain activities?

Asset Rate Curve

What It Is

A visualization of the key assets that drive the majority of an organization's value and their time frames of competitive relevance.

What It Provides

Insights into the rate at which key capabilities, or assets, decrease or increase their value over time—a simple visualization to get executives to *step above* their day-to-day activities and reevaluate the core assets that drive value for their business.

Why It Matters

Organizations deliver products and/or services to their customers (or constituents for public organizations) that these customers care about. Products and services are made up of specific capabilities—whether software, processes, information, or insight. We call these *assets* because they form the foundation of value, however defined, that the organization delivers. For insurance and investment firms, for example, a key asset is their capability to price risk, which underlies the products and services they deliver to their customers. For Walmart, a key asset is their logistics capabilities to provide low-cost products globally. Two of Converse's key assets are their brand and design of youthful rebellion and self-expression that their Chuck Taylor sneakers represent.

- Every organization, no matter how complex and how many products and services they deliver, has only a handful of assets that make up the majority of the value they deliver (fewer than seven). Again, back to insurance or investment firms, every one of their dozens, if not hundreds, of products rests on algorithms and methods to price risk. As technologies evolve, regulations shift, and customer expectations change, the ongoing relevance of these assets change—whether the specific risk profiles (for insurance and investment firms), the software to orchestrate millions of pallets or monitor trucks (for Walmart), or the design relevance of Converse. These assets decay over time. They become less relevant or require significant investments to maintain their relevance. They decay, or accelerate, at different rates. Insight into what these rates are helps to—

- Isolate what changes the slope of its line—i.e., its decay rate and its accompanying inflection points—both activities you control and those you don't

- Identify whether, when, and how much to invest in the asset to maintain its relevance

- Tee up a discussion about what to do with the asset to maintain its relevance—e.g., buy, build, or sell more or less of the asset

- Identify new core assets to invest in

Questions It Helps Answer

What is the decay/acceleration rate of the five to seven assets that drive 70 percent of your value today/tomorrow? What activities are changing those rates? Which of these activities can you control and which can you not control? What do you want to do with the changing assets? Invest in them more? Divest them? Mitigate the risk of their decline through partnership or other mechanisms?

The New 20 Percent, Roles to Perform, and Activities That Shape Ecosystems

Dylan Garnett, the CEO of Metropolitan Health we met in Chapter 2, was fond of saying, "PowerPoint is nice, but execution is key." The models described earlier focused on insight into new sources of value. Insight is nice, but taking action on that insight is critical to capturing new sources of value in new ways. The following set of models help focus and prioritize such action. In short, it's one thing to know what's going on; it's another to do something about it.

Questions to Ask and Answer

How do you shape, influence, or just plain *fit* into an ecosystem to capture new sources of value in new ways? What role(s) do you play within it and what capabilities—the new 20 percent—do you bring to the table to do so?

The New 20 Percent Framework

What It Is

A visual image identifying the new 20 percent of capabilities (assets, skill sets, competencies) critical if you want to capture new sources of value.

What It Provides

A framework to help executives clarify new capabilities to capture new sources of growth.

Why It Matters

Organizations consist of sets of capabilities orchestrated to meet market, customer, or constituent needs. This orchestration consists of different activities and processes conducted by leadership vision and direction setting. Organizations vary in size and complexity. However, irrespective of size and complexity, the value they deliver rests on only a small set of core capabilities. Other capabilities and the activities that surround them are in service of delivering, protecting, and extending the value of the core capabilities. The core capabilities of insurance companies, for example, lie in pricing risk; those of fashion lie in design for a selected set of consumers. As the world changes—driven by shifts in technology, customer, and business models—the core capabilities change.

Take the example we've used previously of the insurance executive who is exploring what happens as their core asset shifts from pricing risk

to preventing accidents, thus requiring a new 20 percent of critical capabilities. Insight into what the new 20 percent may be is critical, as it—

- Distills which core capabilities are critical to capturing new
  sources of value
- Highlights interdependencies among the capabilities in terms
  of how they support each other to create value

Questions It Helps Answer

What is the 20 percent of critical capabilities to capture new sources of
value? How do these capabilities impact each other? How does insight
into this new 20 percent impact the role you play within an ecosystem? And how do you orchestrate capabilities from your ecosystem to
strengthen this new 20 percent?

Business Ecosystem Canvas

What It Is

A depiction of essential elements that make up different types of business ecosystems and specific opportunities to pursue from an ecosystem
perspective.

What It Provides

A snapshot into core elements that make up the specific type of business
ecosystem, and your role within it.

Why It Matters

The business ecosystem canvas shares an objective with the business canvas: to clarify the essence of an opportunity. Many organizations face a challenge to develop and use a shared language to make sense and take action
on specific opportunities, or challenges. We all know the issue: people from
different parts of the organization may use the same language; they certainly hear the same strategic objectives and priorities. Yet what they hear

gets interpreted, filtered, through their own perspectives and processes. The result? Challenges in coordination and execution across different parts of an organization. This is why *execution alignment* has been and will continue to be a challenge for nearly every organization everywhere.[67]

The Business Canvas has become an important, simple tool to clarify the value proposition of specific business opportunities.[68] It seeks to distill the essence of the value proposition around which people with inevitably different perspectives can argue. Such arguments and discussions help folks focus on what it is they need to do.

The Business Canvas's focus is on a specific opportunity, from the perspective of a department or specific business. The Business Ecosystem Canvas shares an objective with the Business Canvas: to clarify the essence of an opportunity. However, its perspective is of the ecosystem opportunity and the role an organization can play within it. They complement each other: similar structure, same objective, different perspective. The ecosystem canvas helps a business to—

- Distill the core value proposition of an opportunity, *from an ecosystem perspective*

- Clarify the mechanics of how the business ecosystem is orchestrated

- Compare which type of ecosystem is relevant for specific opportunities

- Highlight the different roles that organizations can play within different types of ecosystems

---

67   This was written about extensively in our second book. See Ralph Welborn and Vince Kasten, *Get It Done! A Blueprint for Business Execution* (New York: Wiley, 2005). We focused on what we called the *semantic disconnects* that exist among different types of leaders and departments. These disconnects are rational and to be expected. People from different parts of an organization have different perspectives and ways of getting done what needs to get done. How many times have you been in meetings where you heard someone say, "Well, that's not my understanding of what was said or needed to be done"? If not many times, then you are in the minority. People from different parts of an organization speak, or at least understand, things differently, hence the ongoing challenge to get alignment around priorities and activities that executives may think are clear but in reality aren't. Sensitive leaders understand this challenge of semantic disconnects. They work hard to build a common language—one that makes sense differently to the different folks who make up and run the business.

68   Alexander Osterwalder and Yves Pigneur, *Business Model Generation* (New York: John Wiley & Sons, 2010).

Reference Architectures
What It Is
Reference architectures are visual depictions of business and technology capabilities.

What It Provides
Depiction of business and/or technology and/or data architecture underlying the journey/road map.

Why It Matters
Reference architectures clarify what folks are talking about and the effects different projects will have on different parts of the business. They also clarify who within one's ecosystem performs what set of activities, which is helpful in understanding how decisions and actions impact each other.

Organizations consist of people, processes, and activities with different sets of responsibilities and ways of doing what needs to get done. As many have highlighted, they "talk a different language"—e.g., business folks look at the business differently than technology folks (in general); they have different training, experience, responsibilities, and often different ways of looking at the same set of activities. A challenge for many organizations is building a common language—or at least a way to communicate with different sets of people in ways that talk their own language but is understandable to others so that they can be more aligned in terms of executing more effectively.[69] Many organizations have technology reference architectures; fewer have business reference architectures. Yet they are complements to each other. Changes in one may have implications for the other. Consequently, they are pragmatic, and simple, frameworks to help clarify who does what and how actions from one team impact those on another. This is important within any business, and critical when dealing with orchestrating capabilities from different organizations.

---

69   Welborn and Kasten, *Get It Done!*

Questions It Helps Answer

What are the key activities that make up the business and technology sides of the organization? How do changes in these activities impact other activities? Which of these activities make up the new 20 percent of critical capabilities? What do we do with the rest of them—in terms of investment, maintenance, and support? Which of these are provided by partners, and when?

Section 2: Journey Maps as a Series of "Aha" Moments

The beginning of this chapter brought together different models for visualizing and understanding aspects of business ecosystems.

In this section, we take three different types of projects, each with a different objective, but all designed to capture new sources of value within an ecosystem. We walk through them illustrating how the models described earlier can be used to construct each of these journeys.

We selected these three particular examples for pragmatic reasons. First, they focus on different—but common—types of questions that many organizations are seeking to answer. Second, they reflect different sponsors within an organization. And third, they reflect different time frames of execution. These three different types of examples are—

- A health insurance company's digital transformation, with its core objective to identify and claim new sources of value

- A consumer product company with its core objective to design a new consumer engagement model critical to growing three times that of the industry average

- A manufacturing company seeking to optimize its R&D and innovation portfolio around a big bet—clarifying whether its portfolio is pointed in the right direction and how to speed getting results from it once it is

The objective for the rest of this chapter is not to go into the details of these examples. Instead, it lies in suggesting how these journeys can be constructed from the models that guide them.

A Digital Transformation Journey

The following image depicts a strategic journey for a global health insurance company. The objective underlying this journey was clear: to identify and catalyze new sources of value. The challenges were also clear: margins were under pressure; revenue growth had slipped to the industry average; new types of competitors were nibbling away at different profit pools; and investment focus was helping the top, but not the bottom, line. Doing more of the same was not an option.

Significant investments in digital capabilities across the industry—the CLAMS (cloud, location, analytics, mobile, and social)—were resulting in an investment race among traditional competitors without any clear breakthrough strategic or execution plan. This is not an uncommon situation. Let's walk through the models this health insurance company used to change the game during the four phases making up the journey, which were—

1. Clarify where value was being created and destroyed in the company's ecosystem
2. Identify potential sources of new foundations of value
3. Design new methods to engage customers, stakeholders, and markets

   This phase raised (as it always does) significant opportunities for customers and stakeholders to engage, products and services to design, capabilities (the new 20 percent) to develop, governance to rethink, and business models to evolve.
4. Launch quickly, to test out the new model, supported by an execution plan to scale, with speed

DIGITAL TRANSFORMATION JOURNEY

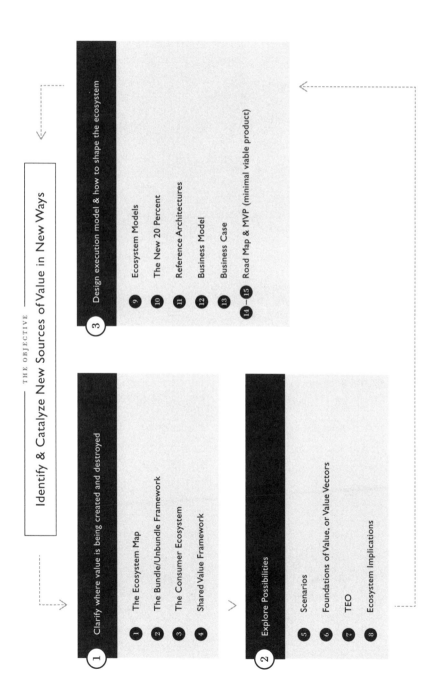

THE OBJECTIVE

Identify & Catalyze New Sources of Value in New Ways

1 Clarify where value is being created and destroyed

- ① The Ecosystem Map
- ② The Bundle/Unbundle Framework
- ③ The Consumer Ecosystem
- ④ Shared Value Framework

2 Explore Possibilities

- ⑤ Scenarios
- ⑥ Foundations of Value, or Value Vectors
- ⑦ TEO
- ⑧ Ecosystem Implications

3 Design execution model & how to shape the ecosystem

- ⑨ Ecosystem Models
- ⑩ The New 20 Percent
- ⑪ Reference Architectures
- ⑫ Business Model
- ⑬ Business Case
- ⑭—⑮ Road Map & MVP (minimal viable product)

The four phases are common to many strategy and execution pro-grams; yet the models and methods inside these phases differ. Phase 1 typically answers the question, What's going on and where might we play? Phase 2 answers the question, Where should we play? Phase 3 answers the question, How do we play? And Phase 4 answers the question: How do we start and how do we execute?

Phase 1

Phase 1 was designed to answer one specific question: What's going on within our ecosystem, and where might we focus to capture new sources of value? The first four models of this phase are useful to help answer that question.

#1—The Ecosystem Map

Insight into who the actors are within one's ecosystem establishes the baseline for subsequent decisions about where to focus and whom to engage. Ecosystem maps visually clarify who make up one's ecosystem.

Here's a lesson learned: this is an entertaining exercise to do with your teams. From our experience, everyone scoffs, "Of course, we know who makes up our ecosystem." Initially.

What has always been compelling, based on our experience, is the process of creating the model. It only takes a few minutes to identify the actors. What takes time, and makes the model useful, is asking the next set of questions: What is the relationship among these actors; how is value allocated across them; how might that allocation change given new entrants, technology, regulations, and customer expectations; who are the new entrants coming into this ecosystem; and what is drawing them into it?

Here is where the scoffing stops and the compelling part begins. This map is used later in the process—particularly in Phase 3 when figuring out your execution plan. The questions asked initially are asked again, and the answers clarify how to shape your ecosystem to meet your objectives.

#2—The Bundle/Unbundle Framework

Industries frequently go through cycles of being aggregated and dis-aggregated, or bundled and unbundled. Shifts in technology, business models, regulations, and customer expectations drive these cycles. This framework provides another way to see where profit pools or sources of value are being created or squeezed. Visually displaying this process helps answer questions such as, What is driving these changes? What parts of the value chain are being impacted the most? What new types of actors are engaging in which parts of the value chain? What capabilities are they using? Answers to these questions complement those provided in the ecosystem map. Together they help illustrate where to focus.

#3—The Consumer Ecosystem

Peter Drucker, arguably the first and most influential business strat-egist, once wrote that organizations are merely mechanisms to meet customer and consumer needs. No customers, no business. No surprise here. It is also why so much attention and effort is focused on cus-tomer centricity, segmentation, and journey maps. What is surprising is that much of this customer focus rarely focuses on the customer *from the customer's perspective*. The analogy of the blind men describing an elephant is apt to illustrate this point—as each man describes only a part of the elephant from their individual vantage point, but none can see the whole elephant.

Customer centricity, for many organizations, falls into this blind-man-and-the-elephant trap. They define customers in terms of *magic* or *delight touchpoints*, or segment them into life stages or behavioral demographics. Such segmentation is used to sell products or services at the so-called right price at the right time through the right channel. A footwear company, for example, tends to segment their customers like those above. Revenue growth comes from understanding this seg-mentation and activities to sell more shoes into these segments. Growth will be a multiple of the apparel industry growth and market share into these segments. This would be a fine approach—*if* the competitive landscape hadn't changed and new business models hadn't emerged. But they have.

This model explores the ecosystem from the perspective of the consumer. It doesn't look at the behavioral characteristics of the consumer with respect to your products or services. Instead, it focuses on where, when, and how the consumer spends their time, energy, and resources irrespective of product or service. This insight is useful to ask questions such as, What does the consumer care about as measured by time, energy, and resources *that they* expend? What are the products and services that make up where, when, and how your consumer engages? What do those ecosystems look like? What are the opportunities for you to engage in those ecosystems? What would be the capabilities—and new products and services—required to meet the outcomes and expectations the customer has for what they are doing?

This model provides an *outside-in* focus on what consumers care about. This focus turns the typical set of questions around and asks how what it is you do *fits into* what consumers care about rather than how what they do fits into your set of products and services.

#4—Shared Value Framework

Different actors are motivated by different types of value. The shared value framework maps what these different types of value are and who cares about them. The range of ecosystem players in this project was extensive. It ranged from health care regulators to clinicians, from telecommunications companies to logistics providers, from global IT services firms to local media companies. What each of these parties cared about was as varied as the industries they came from. A shared value framework was critical to start bringing them together. It became a pragmatic tool to keep them focused and eventually aligned around what each party brought to the table.

Phase 2

Phase 1 answered the question, What's going on and where might we play? Phase 2 is designed to answer the question, Where should we play?

#5—Scenarios

It was uncertain how different parties would be impacted by the health system transformation. It was equally uncertain what type of external activities would impact the shape of the new health system. Building scenarios is one way to reduce such uncertainties. Executing the same way knowing that one's competitive environment is changing strategically makes no sense. Doing nothing is equally nonsensical. But what do you do in an uncertain environment other than what you've done before? One pragmatic step, of course, is to build *agile* capabilities to allow you to respond to whatever happens. A second is to build a series of scenarios based on critical actions and assumptions that, should they come to pass, will impact you in different ways.

Scenarios allow you to play *what if* games. Also called *possible futures* or *world-building*, scenarios are pragmatic steps to build a common language about what's possible and what you might do within those worlds. They can take a number of forms: Monte Carlo–driven scenarios are software-enabled simulations. The power of using them lies in the flexibility and number of simulations you can run. Change your assumptions about what key activities might happen—e.g., changes in the price of energy, regulatory policy in the European Union (EU), automation impact on employment in a particular region, adoption rate of a certain technology, or whatever—and run the simulations multiple times. The result? A probability distribution of possible futures that you can manipulate. Immersive games or interactive videos are another form of scenarios. Their power lies in their immersive, visceral capabilities. Powerful games or videos *throw you* into the story line, creating as much of an emotional response as an analytic one. Other types of scenarios exist. They all serve the same purposes, to

- Explore where *future-back opportunities meet present-forward capabilities*
- Build a common language among your executive team around what might happen and steps to take depending on what does happen

What makes these scenarios pragmatic, rather than merely compelling, is when they incorporate the information discovered in Phase 1 and combine it with that of Phase 2. For this particular project, we explored *what if* scenarios around effects on different organizations and how they might be impacted if the government decided to nationalize the health system or not, the implications of a faster or slower adoption of tele-medicine capabilities, implications of greater or lesser employment in other sectors of the economy, and so on. Such exploration helped the executive team align around what could happen and what role they might perform within differing possible worlds, and what capabilities they would need.

#6—*Foundations of Value, or Value Vectors*

Businesses are frequently optimized for a world that no longer exists. As technologies, regulations, and consumer expectations change, so too do the sources of value that organizations and industries deliver.

Earlier we used an example of new foundations of value impacting the retail industry. Yesterday's landscape was shaped by convenience and speed to the consumer's home; these remain critical key sources of value (and differentiation). A new value vector (to use a jargony term) or foundation exists, as demonstrated by Amazon—that of predictive insight. For health care, the value vectors are affordability, access, and outcomes. Hundreds, if not thousands, of activities are important, if not critical. Yet all of them are in service of delivering the health-care foundations of value. This model forces a discussion around the essential sources of value. It distills what comes out of the scenarios in terms of what value is created and thereby suggests what to focus on.

The blunt reality is that it's easy for organizations to get wrapped up in the details of their operations and lose the big picture of what it is that truly drives their growth and how changes in their ecosystem shape that growth. Take the example here: aligning around the foundations of affordability, access, and outcomes reclarified the focus of the executive team around what had made them successful to date—identifying where challenges were coming from and prioritizing where to focus. As such, these new foundations served as a filter—or criteria—to make decisions around where to focus, the capabilities needed, and the role to play within a shifting ecosystem.

#7—TEO

TEO quantifies the economic and/or social benefit to be realized from what the organization has learned as a result of viewing their industry or consumers from an ecosystem perspective.

Defining economic opportunity from a health-system—or any industry—perspective is straightforward. Look at the spend, the cost, the customers (patients), the growth rate, and other key variables and then figure out what your specific opportunity is under a set of assumptions. The problem with this approach is that industries converge—i.e., they are impacted by new types of entrants, technologies, customer expectations, and consequently opportunities. Defining opportunity from a TEO is always different from that of a traditional assessment perspective—not necessarily larger, just different. The shift toward redefining the automobile ecosystem from a transportation to a mobility one is an example—bringing in new players, capabilities, and revenue opportunities (and challenges), different from the traditional way of looking at one's competitive environment. Health systems are no different. The TEO underlying the example we're highlighting here required as much consideration into content management, digital distribution, logistics, and mobile/data capabilities as on the traditional boundaries of health system organizations and capabilities. Clarifying what the TEO was helped the various stakeholders engaged in the project figure out where they should focus, and combined with some of the other models discussed, where and how to do so.

#8—Ecosystem Implications

Change creates new winners and losers. The models of Phase 2 provide insight into the social and economic implications of change, from an eco-system perspective. So it's only logical that the insights on Phase 2 will suggest new ways for you to look at your ecosystem, taking us back to review the first model of the journey.

We mentioned before that many of these models get reused. Each answers a specific question. All provide a specific insight from a different vantage point. The output of some serves as input into others. This par-ticular ecosystem map is a variation of the first one, informed by previous models. Again, why does this matter? Because an ecosystem perspective requires new ways of thinking about what is going on and what you might do about it. That the models build upon and inform each other helps to build a new language. From this perspective, we think of these models as grammar tools—parts of speech that you use over and over again to create a new shared language around how to identify and capture new sources of value.

Phase 3

Whereas Phase 2 helped clarify what the new sources of value were, Phase 3 answers the next logical question: How do we capture it?

#9—Ecosystem Models

Different types of business ecosystems exist. You can visually map what these differences are; this helps clarify which ones are relevant to you, given your objectives. It also helps you explore what roles you might perform within them.

#10—The New 20 Percent

We've spent much time talking about the new 20 percent of capabilities critical to capturing new sources of value. The capabilities that made you successful yesterday (and today) will not be the same as those needed tomorrow. We quoted the insurance executive's comment about the new 20 percent earlier: "Insurance is based on the core capability of pricing and managing risk . . . What happens when we move from a world of pricing risk to one whereby the critical capability is preventing accidents? This is a world we're going to. And we're not sure what to do about it." The underlying questions of Phase 1 and 2 help to provide part of this answer. Models 9 and 10 answer another part—namely, to clarify what those capabilities are and how to start migrating to them. Decisions about new capabilities always raise considerations of what to do about the (previously new or) existing (old?) capabilities. A key question becomes, How do you start to migrate toward these new capabilities while mitigating the risks of doing so—given that you have an organization that has been successful to date? The new 20 percent model helps to answer the first part of this question, while Model 11 begins to answer the second part.

#11—*Reference Architectures*

Digital transformation involves the integration of the CLAMS into existing business and technology environments. The new 20 percent of capabilities require you to articulate what these new capabilities are and clarify their consequences on the business and technology sides of an organization.

   Business and technology architectures complement each other. Business architectures visually depict the functions that underlie the business; technology architectures visually depict the technical capabilities that do so. They are two sides of the same coin: different engravings but joined together. You can't have one side without the other. These *reference* architectures *refer* to different perspectives of the business. What happens in one of the architectures can be traced to the other side. This tracing helps to communicate the business value of technology and the technology implications of business decisions. Both are critical to figuring out the implications of the new 20 percent and implications of the roles to be played in the ecosystem that you decide. Like each of the models, they are communication tools. They can be used, like the children's book *Where's Waldo*, to point to the parts of the architectures you will impact and the parts that will be addressed by other members within the ecosystem. We cannot overemphasize the criticality of these models—to support Dave's admonition.

#12—Business Model

Business models are a fancy phrase for a simple idea. They reflect different ways to orchestrate capabilities to meet consumer needs. Ecosystem-centric business models are those that orchestrate capabilities from different actors to do the same. Shaping one's ecosystem requires insights into what that ecosystem is and where to focus.

All of the previous models described serve as inputs into this model. This one helps answer questions such as, How will we engage with customers differently? What are the core interactions to do so? How do we support a multisided relationship with consumers—helping them become both consumers and producers in the production of value? What will be the balance among products and services to support this new engagement model? What do services even mean in a product company and products in a services one? What will be the implications for revenue and pricing, engagement and investments, and so on?

#13—Business Case

This model brings back the shared value model, extending the typical way organizations define business cases under different conditions. What's new here is the addition of the shared value perspectives and figuring out how to capture different types of value. An ecosystem-centric business case involves figuring out what works for you and what works for others within the ecosystem. This case gets input from Models 1, 2, 4, 5, and 7.

#14 and #15—Road Map and MVP (Minimal Viable Product)

These are typical outputs of just about any project that wants to drive execution. These focus on staging projects and launching new capabilities through some sort of pilot or MVP.

Summary

The phases that this health insurance company took in their digital transformation journey are similar to other transformation journeys. The models depict the navigation posts along the way. We often depict journeys according to the models used for three reasons:

- They represent the key questions that need to be answered.

- They depict the outputs to do so. We find focusing on outputs rather than activities to be more insightful for decision makers as they seek to understand what they will get, when.

- They help clarify what those navigation guideposts are and consequently help to build a common language about what needs to get done, how to do so, and what you get along the way.

A different company may use different models in their transformation journey. The example used is but one of many that we could have described. The intent here is to suggest how you might start using the insights discussed throughout the book to design your journey from an ecosystem perspective. The next example draws from a different client in a different industry. The objective here was less to build out a full-blown digital transformation strategy than to design a new consumer engagement and business model to support consumers in new ways.

Design of a New Consumer Engagement Model

Our second example depicts the journey of a client in a different industry. A Fortune 150 company, one of the most well-recognized and creative brands across the globe, needed to create a new method to engage their consumers. Industry growth was in low single digits worldwide. Their stock price had been relatively flat for years. They were facing new entrants coming into their space. Their customers were demanding more engagement through digital channels. Though they were responding to these demands, so too were their competitors. In short, they were doing what nearly everyone else in their industry was doing—not an approach to create distinctive or explosive growth. Their objective was to figure out how to do so. What we'll describe below is a part of the project—to figure out how to engage with customers in new ways, in the ecosystems in which they engaged, as a possible means to stop running the Red Queen race.

The phases are similar to the digital transformation journey:

1. Clarify where value is being created and destroyed within your and your customer's ecosystem.
2. Design a new consumer engagement model around what they care about—e.g., as potential new sources of value to capture.
3. Design an execution program to engage with your consumers in new ways.

We use this example for two reasons.

First, it's a common challenge. As Peter Drucker once wrote, organizations exist only to serve the needs of their customers, or constituents. No customers, no business; no constituents, no organizations. Yet, customer expectations change, and such changes always impact different parts of a value chain. The implication? The bundling and unbundling of industries as new types of actors enter different parts of a value chain and existing ones concentrate their attention in others.

Let's make this tangible with an example.

Technology capabilities have changed the economics of many steps within many value chains. Electronic distribution, to take but one example, has slashed the margins of what was once a high-margin business in the media business. The place for profits shifted from distribution to customer service. Those who owned the eyeballs owned the greatest source of (potential) profit. At the same time, the marginal cost of acquiring customers dropped nearly to zero. The result? Recognition that the source of content was less important than its aggregation and engagement with customers. The implication? Media consolidation (i.e., bundling) around customer engagement and fragmentation (i.e., unbundling) of content creation and production.

The lesson to take from this example? Profit pools change. These changes provide insight into what customers care about—from a rearview mirror perspective. They provide insight into what has already changed. What you need is to get some foresight into where new profit pools are likely to be created. The ecosystem models and the first phase of this journey help to do that. These models can be used to figure out new ways to engage your customers in the ecosystems that they care about, rather than how you have defined them to care about your products or services.

Second, the models used for the digital transformation journey are similar to those underlying this journey. This is clear by looking through the following figure. Again, models are merely mechanisms to help you answer new types of questions in new ways. The upshot? Use the ones that are useful to meet the objectives you have.

Since this journey is similar to the previous one, we won't walk through each of the steps. However, there are two points to highlight.

First, the order of the models differs slightly. This reflects the differing objective and scope of the project. Second, this company had significant materials from consultants, research firms, their internal marketing efforts, and outputs of R&D investments. Having this material was helpful. It allowed the journey to go that much faster.

Ecosystem-centric questions are like the Hubble Telescope, which sheds new light on the same set of activities. Much of the data that astronomers had collected prior to the launch of the Hubble Telescope remained useful. Insights drawn from it were different both because new types of data were added to the existing set and new insights shed new light on how to make use of existing data. The same happens with much of the sunk costs of time, energy, and resources you already have. It also makes the buy-in from your stakeholders easier. We spoke of "aha" moments previously—whereby new insights may trigger folks to see new patterns or insights. Seeing how existing information gets used in new ways helps speed the buy-in critical to exploiting novel insights.

Not every organization has the luxury that this global brand does. However, the point remains the same, irrespective of size: use what you

CONSUMER ENGAGEMENT JOURNEY

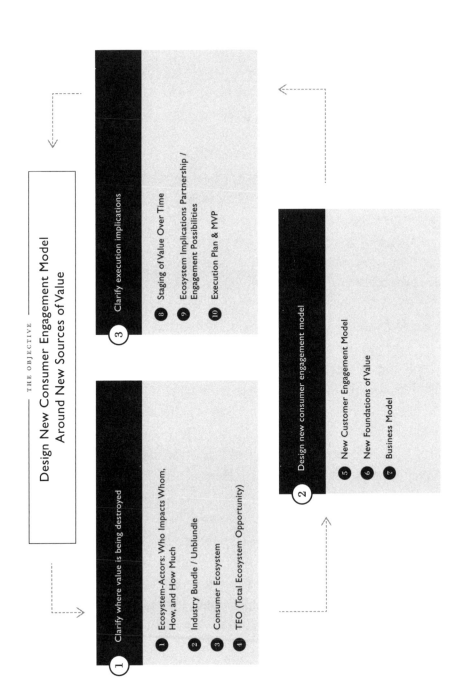

THE OBJECTIVE
Design New Consumer Engagement Model Around New Sources of Value

1 Clarify where value is being destroyed

1 Ecosystem-Actors: Who Impacts Whom, How, and How Much
2 Industry Bundle / Unbundle
3 Consumer Ecosystem
4 TEO (Total Ecosystem Opportunity)

2 Design new consumer engagement model

5 New Customer Engagement Model
6 New Foundations of Value
7 Business Model

3 Clarify execution implications

8 Staging of Value Over Time
9 Ecosystem Implications Partnership / Engagement Possibilities
10 Execution Plan & MVP

have. What's unique here is the set of new types of questions asked. Much of the information, research, and data you have will be helpful. The challenge lies in the initial set of questions and the process to work through. Changing the unit of focus from any particular business or industry to the ecosystem in which you are engaged is the jujitsu shift that needs to happen. The core philosophy of that martial art rests on using the energy and strength you already have in new ways. Little movements have large impacts. So it is with our recommended process. Use what you have. Ask different questions. Change the unit of focus. As you do so, much like any newly colored lens, you see the same things in different ways. That's what these journeys are all about—making visible what is invisible in terms of where new sources of value are being created and how to capture them.

The result of this project? Early returns on the revised program—consisting of new programs to engage customers, rearticulation of new foundations of value, a focus on a new 20 percent of capabilities, and programs both to engage their ecosystem and that of their customers—are suggesting a growth rate of 3.5 times that of the industry average.

Getting More Out of Your Innovation (and R&D) Portfolio

This third journey differs from the other two. It had two clear objectives: to validate that their R&D portfolio was pointed in the right direction (toward explosive growth opportunities) and to figure out how to capture those opportunities faster.

Many organizations have a portfolio of different types of investments: (a) incremental; (b) those adjacent to the core business; and (c) those that could change the game, either in terms of the amount of net new revenue it brings in or a dramatic change in the business model. This third journey is the latter. It is based on an organization with an innovation portfolio covering all three types of objectives: incremental, adjacent, and breakthrough.

The journey we'll walk through focuses on their big bet—i.e., disruptive—objective. However, the process is relevant to the other types as well. Some different types of models were used for this journey. However, what underlines the process and the specific models remains the same: an ecosystem perspective and the criticality of answering the new strategic questions.

The overall objective for this organization's journey was clear: to increase the likelihood that their breakthrough portfolio would be successful. They had well over one hundred projects that made up their big bet. They had specific questions to answer: Do we have the right portfolio? Is it pointed in the right direction? When are we likely to realize value? What kind of value might be realized under different future scenarios? How can we accelerate realizing that value? And overall, how can we get a faster and bigger return on our big-bet investments?

The project was divided into three phases.

- Phase 1 focused on one core question: What is the TEO—the total ecosystem opportunity—underlying the portfolio? This question had to be answered for two reasons: first, to determine if they were focused on the right big-bet opportunities; second, to figure out if they had the right set of projects to work on.

- Phase 2 had one core question to answer as well: What different types of value could be realized from the opportunity defined, and how does that value get distributed across both the projects and the ecosystem partners critical to capturing them?

- The models used in Phase 1 were the same as the starting points for the other two journeys discussed. The questions underlying Phase 2 were answered largely through simulation. Simulations test assumptions and activities. They are an effective way to explore the ripple effects of decisions made and actions taken. They also help to explore how projects that make up a portfolio impact each other under different conditions, which is precisely what we need when we take an ecosystem perspective.

- Getting insight into how decisions made and actions taken will ripple throughout a network is an important skill when working

INNOVATION PORTFOLIO JOURNEY

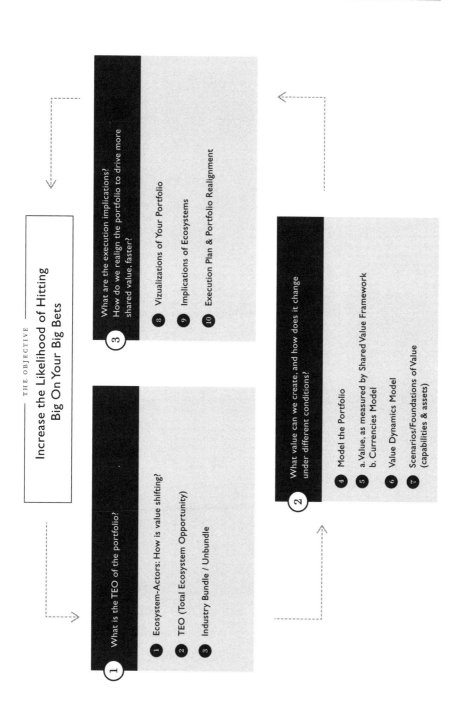

THE OBJECTIVE
Increase the Likelihood of Hitting
Big On Your Big Bets

1 What is the TEO of the portfolio?

1 Ecosystem-Actors: How is value shifting?

2 TEO (Total Ecosystem Opportunity)

3 Industry Bundle / Unbundle

2 What value can we create, and how does it change under different conditions?

4 Model the Portfolio

5 a. Value, as measured by Shared Value Framework
b. Currencies Model

6 Value Dynamics Model

7 Scenarios/Foundations of Value (capabilities & assets)

3 What are the execution implications?
How do we realign the portfolio to drive more shared value, faster?

8 Vizualizations of Your Portfolio

9 Implications of Ecosystems

10 Execution Plan & Portfolio Realignment

within ecosystems. Simulations help strengthen that skill. Change an activity, and see how it ripples throughout the network; change the cost of labor or capital or energy or introduce a certain technology, and observe how it impacts who wins and loses in terms of value created. The models underlying Phase 2 were inputs for the simulations. Phase 3 focused on the core question of how to get more out of the portfolio faster. Whereas Phase 2 was largely supported by simulations, Phase 3's core question was answered by different types of data visualizations. The first three models have been described earlier. They were starting points for the other two journeys discussed. We'll start with Model #4, the portfolio model.

#4—The Portfolio Model

The portfolio model captures information about the innovation or R&D portfolio. It is depicted here as a visualization or a chart. This image is based on a worksheet (or simple database) capturing characteristics of each of the 100+ projects underlying the so-called big bet. These characteristics create a standard set of data within the portfolio that can be input into both the simulation and data visualizations.

#5a and #5b—The Shared Value Framework and Currencies Model

We've discussed this model earlier. Different actors within an ecosystem care about different types of value. Currencies reflect different types of value that motivate the behavior of different actors.

Both the shared value framework and the currencies model formalize the different types of value that different actors care about. The shared value framework helps to build out an ecosystem-centric balance sheet. Such a sheet helps when you want to figure out who the new winners and losers may be under different conditions. The currency model helps to visualize the different types of value—in this example, profit, sustainability, or brand equity—by sets of projects, programs, different scenarios, and ecosystem actors.

#6—*Value Dynamics Model*

This model distills the key activities that increase or decrease a particular type of value that you care about. For example, if revenue growth is driven by the number of widgets you sell, then this model identifies the key activities that interact to drive sales. Multiple activities interact, creating a tapestry of both positive and negative feedback loops to drive sales. This model teases apart those interactions. It distills which ones have positive and which have negative impacts on those sales. These activities become central inputs for the simulation.

#7—*Scenarios/Possible Worlds*

Simulations provide a probability distribution of different types of value that you may realize under different conditions based on decisions made and actions taken. They are an effective way to isolate key activities that could have large impacts on your entire portfolio.

Big bets tend to take time to come to fruition. Lots can happen in an extended time frame: regulations change, technological advances, labor policy shifts, etc. For this project, we isolated several external variables and ran multiple scenarios against them to help figure out the implications for the big-bet portfolio, given changes beyond the control of this company. We also ran simulations based on different decisions the company might make. Again, the focus of the project was to ensure that the portfolio was focused in the right place (as opportunities change) and to figure out how to accelerate realizing the value from it. Scenarios were important to help answer this first question.

#8—*Visualizations of your Portfolio*

Projects impact each other. They also impact stakeholders. Visualizing these interdependencies is helpful in several ways. First, it clarifies what the most important projects are. Importance here may not necessarily be the largest or the riskiest. It simply means the most *connected* in that other projects are dependent on it being successful. A variety of different type of visualizations are useful. The first is what is known as a node-linked diagram, depicting how multiple objects are linked together. For this project, we created a visualization consisting of different colored balls (projects) linked together in different ways. Each of these dots represents a project within the big-bet portfolio; the different colors represent groupings of those projects.

An "aha" moment occurred when we all first saw this visualization. It told a surprising story: the complex, well over one hundred projects that made up this portfolio were dependent on four projects. These four projects, three from different programs, were central to the other projects being effective. If they failed, or were delayed, the entire project timing, budget, and likelihood of impact would be impacted. A second type of visualization extends this analysis—mapping the projects both to each other (e.g., which ones are related to which ones) as well as to the various stakeholders (e.g., who is or should be involved in which projects). A third visualization we commonly use is called a Sankey diagram. It depicts dependencies across the projects by degree of risk and timing. It provides yet another perspective on which projects and their underlying capabilities are critical to meeting the objectives of your program. For each of these visualizations, you can select—grab—any of the nodes, pick it up or move it around, and explore how the interdependencies of the projects change. This ability to manipulate these visualizations provides another way to explore how you might speed up execution or reduce risk of your overall program.

Key to data visualizations is making visible what is invisible. Ecosystems, by definition, extend our typical way of viewing our competitive landscape. The combination of simulations plus visualizations helps us see beyond what we typically do. Both help isolate key activities—and capabilities. Both also help create a shared language among folks with different perspectives in two ways:

- First, they allow you to see what happens when you change the quantity or quality of certain of these activities. What happens to the entire portfolio and ecosystem, for example, when the price of energy rises, you invest more in local manufacturing capability, technology adoption is not as fast as you thought, or whatever?

- Second, you can tease apart the (often) complex interactions of multiple projects within your portfolio. Such visualizations clarify the key processes and capabilities critical to your overall program.

We are all story-telling animals. Many of us are visually sensitive, with insight coming from storybook-like visualizations and the capability to manipulate them. Changing the unit of focus to the ecosystem suggests that we need new ways to both tell that story and make sense of our role within it. The models underlying this journey help us to do so.

#9 and #10—Ecosystem Implications and Portfolio Realignment (Execution Plan)

These models helped us figure out how to engage the ecosystem of the big-bet portfolio and the execution plan to engage it: model 9 explored the effects on the ecosystem of the insights gained; model 10 depicted the realignment of the portfolio as a result of the journey undertaken.

Summary

What was the result? A refocus of where the company wanted to focus and realignment among all of the executives—and a reconfiguration of the R&D portfolio based on insight as to where, how, and when to capture the new sources of value they intended to capture.

In Closing: Cross the Rubicon

Other journeys could have been described and other models used. The purpose of this chapter is to provide a few examples of how you might put together a number of the insights discussed throughout this book— in a pragmatic way.

In 49 BC, Caesar crossed the Rubicon and burned his boats. "There is no going back," he told his army. "The world has changed and we must find new ways to act within it." The same holds true regarding our new competitive landscape. Technological shifts have seen to that.

Technological advances have always outpaced our organizational and managerial capabilities to understand both their implications and how to harness them. The rise of the CLAMS has catalyzed new forms of engagement, creating a tapestry of many-to-many relationships. The exploding use of virtual, augmented, or multimodel reality is creating new methods of engaging with each other and of how we learn. The rise of machine intelligence and what Kevin Kelly describes as "different types of intelligence" will require us to figure out new ways to engage both with each other and with organizations to meet social and economic needs we have.

The upshot? We are in the early days of knowing what tomorrow will bring. What we do know, however, is that much like Caesar's burning of his boats at the Rubicon, the world has changed and there's no going back.

Back to the purpose of this chapter. Making practical how to engage your ecosystem requires recognizing two things: first, that your competitive landscape has changed and that ecosystem-centric business models are the natural evolution of these changes. Second, that these new business models are based on new strategic questions, answers which have very real implications for—

- Customers to engage (in new ways)
- (New sources of) value to create
- The new 20 percent of critical capabilities to do so
- Ecosystems to shape

The examples and methods described in this chapter have hopefully provided suggestions of how to identify and capture new sources of value in new ways. Those who can see and close the gap between technology shifts and our managerial capabilities will always be the winners within a new competitive landscape. Describing the journeys and the models that help navigate them in this chapter is our attempt to help you begin to close that gap faster, thereby positioning you today as one of the winners of tomorrow.

8

And Now What?

Brian, senior vice president of policy and new markets at one of the world's largest pharmaceutical companies, had a challenge. The explosion of health-related devices and information sources, delivered as needed and whenever desired, reflected the simplicity of interactions customers had come to expect in many other parts of their lives—for example, quick delivery from Amazon and instant rides with Uber. Customers now expected similar easy transactions with those engaged in delivering their health-care services, including pharmaceutical companies. It was clear that what customers cared about regarding health care was broader than what Brian and his pharmaceutical company were focused on. How they had been engaging with their customers was different from how their customers needed or wanted to engage. The question was how to do so, and what consequences such changes would have on their market differentiation, competition, and fundamental value proposition. The company's market cap and growth rate had been, like many of the largest pharmaceutical companies, growing fine—in the range of 4 to 5 percent CAGR since 2011. This was clearly less by nearly 50 percent of the average biotech firm, but it was respectable.

Business Ecosystems as Tomorrow's Engines of Explosive Growth

The challenge for Brian's firm lay in what they saw as "clouds on the horizon"—namely, shifts in customer expectations, regulatory policy, and technological advances. "How might these shifts affect how we engage with customers and our partners?" was one of the questions Brian and his team posed. Another was, "What might our competitive landscape look like in five-plus years?"

We worked through these questions, starting with a discussion of two different movies: *Blade Runner* and *The Social Network*. *Blade Runner*, a cult classic movie from 1982, reflects a world dominated by enormous companies, a dystopic view of an us-versus-them perspective of the world—a zero-sum game based on the premise of the bigger-the-business-the-better, where the more powerful wins. *The Social Network*, which came out in 2010, depicts the origin story of Facebook. Facebook, of course, connects folks into greater and greater circles of interconnectivity and peer-based, so-called friend-based, relationships.

Both movies reflect different perspectives of a former and an emerging competitive world. *Blade Runner* is based on an assumption of control—of the imperative to internalize (or, in business jargon, vertically integrate) as many business activities and transaction costs as possible and thereby deliver services at scale through supply and distribution channels that you control. Sources of differentiation remain based on delivering a *good enough* product at a profitable price with the competitive intent crisply focused on crushing well-defined competitors through measuring the amount of market share you take away from them in a well-defined market.

The Social Network has a vastly different perspective of the competitive landscape. For it, sources of differentiation lie not as much in profitable price and products as in connectivity, enablement, and insight into the changing dynamics of the environment in which your customers engage and the capabilities that mobilize different services and products to support them. It is based on an operational assumption not of control, but its opposite—the adaptability and construction of the conditions to support *whatever* happens. Its premise lies in the statement, "We don't know what will happen, and hence we need to focus on the conditions and capabilities to adapt to rapid changes our customers care about, no matter what happens." Risks, and returns, are shared across the different stakeholders involved in a *Social Network*–envisaged world rather than internalized in that of *Blade Runner*.

We've mentioned several times that businesses are frequently optimized for a world that no longer exists. *The Blade Runner* world is still with us—and will continue to be so, but the world will be increasingly populated by *The Social Network* model and other new business models, driven by ecosystem-centric strategies. The inherent, adaptive nature of capitalism and its engine, the acquisition and delivery of value, will see to that.

"Markets don't work because they are efficient," observes Eric Beinhocker of the New Economy Foundation, "but because they are effective."[70] They provide solutions to problems that customers face. The beauty of commerce lies in the pragmatic explanation that when it works, it rewards people for solving other people's problems.

Let's keep this simple. As we all know, customer desires and expectations change. These changes reflect new possibilities afforded by the complex interplay of technological innovation (you can do new—or more—things in new ways), demographic shifts (placing new types of social and economic pressure where and on what folks care about), regulatory changes (enabling or hindering new types of behaviors), and business models (orchestrating capabilities to serve market needs). Stated differently, these changes are afforded by new sets of capabilities, many of which (most of which?) come from a variety of different sources.

And stated differently again, seldom does any particular company have all the capabilities needed to meet fast-moving customer expectations, desires, or market needs. So what do we need to do organizationally? Change accordingly; adapt to what the changing environment is in which we are engaged, and figure out how to orchestrate the various capabilities to meet those needs. As measured by what? As measured by

70   Beinhocker, *The Origin of Wealth*.

capturing and delivering the types of value that people care about. Businesses, in short, have a simple focus: *capture and deliver value*.

As what counts as value shifts, businesses need to adapt accordingly regarding what they do and how they engage with their customers, markets, and stakeholders.

Selfish Value—as the Engine of Explosive Growth

Business ecosystems are no aberration, nor are they a surprise. They are a natural, adaptive response to shifts in the types of value that folks care about. They reflect patterns of organizational arrangements to both capture and deliver new value in new ways. These new sources of value are catalyzed by the interaction among technology innovation, demographic/behavioral shifts, regulatory changes, and novel business models. Quite the soup of adaptive behavior!

Richard Dawkins is one of the world's most celebrated evolutionary biologists. He is the author of *The Selfish Gene*, a focused book with a provocative, and by now well-accepted, argument—namely, that people are "survival machines—robot vehicles blindly programmed to preserve the selfish molecules known as genes."[71] He argues that the relevant way to understand organisms is to see them as temporary vehicles used to perpetuate DNA.

There has been much debate in a number of fields—from economics, psychology, biology, and philosophy—on how to explain the altruistic behavior of a person, or animal, if they sacrifice themselves for others. Such sacrifice seemingly counters the argument of explaining one's behavior in terms of self-interest in perpetuating one's own genetic line. On the contrary, Dawkins suggests that it is the very selfishness of genes that enables individuals to be selfless. He writes, "The true 'purpose' of [the gene] is to survive, no more and no less."[72] Adaptation reflects the gene's

---

71   Richard Dawkins, *The Selfish Gene: 30th Anniversary Edition* (New York: Oxford University Press, 2006); also, *Brief Candle in the Dark: My Life in Science* (New York: Ecco, 2015).

72   Ibid.

imperative to survive. That species evolve reflects the gene's imperative to survive. And so it is with business and the answer to the question, "Why business ecosystems?"

Businesses are arrangements to capture value. As what counts as value changes, so too must businesses change, or adapt, to survive. Replace the word *gene* with *value* and it becomes clear how and why business ecosystems are merely a logical next step toward how to engage with customers, stakeholders, and markets.

Technology affords new opportunities; regulations create guardrails that serve both to constrain and create opportunities; demographic shifts support new ways of engaging; and the economy reflects the patterned activities of billions of decisions made every day by individuals and organizations. These catalysts—of technology, regulations, demographics, and economic behaviors—reflect the environment in which value gets created—and destroyed—from the perspective of customers and participants. Organizations able to adapt to these changes in value survive; those that can't, don't. From this perspective, deep insight into the types of value that matter to customers—into the market needs, the friction, the breakdown, and the nonconsumption that create explosive opportunities—provide the motor for business model innovation.

Natural Selection and Business Evolution

Back to Dawkins for a moment. Natural selection is blunt: organisms look like and behave as they do because their form and function have evolved or—in biological terms—*have been selected* to ensure the survival of the (selfish) gene. We see this in more than biology. Increasingly, folks are recognizing that the mechanism of change across the board is Darwinian: it is gradual, inexorable, combinatorial, and selective.

Consider music and its evolution. As Matt Ridley writes, "To a surprising extent, [music] changes under its own steam, with musicians carried along for the ride. Baroque begets classical begets romantic begets ragtime begets jazz begets blues begets rock begets pop. One style could not emerge without the previous style existing."[73] A 2015 book on how pop hits are made describes the dramatic economic and organizational changes that have impacted the music industry. It illustrates how hit-making has evolved—from the idea of the solo genius songwriter (like Paul McCartney, John Lennon, George and Ira Gershwin, and so on) to the orchestrator of different types of folks who excel in a specific element critical to producing a great hit. You have specialists who do nothing more than provide the melody, those who lay down the beat and bass line, those whose sole responsibility is to provide what is known as the *bridge* or transition between verses, and even those whose critical role involves creating what are known as musical hooks—the repeatable sounds that serve as hangers, off of which many of the other elements of the song hang (think the "u-u-u-umbrella" hook in Rihanna's multi-platinum song "Umbrella" or Ester Dean's "take it, take it" in her explosive hit, "Rude Boy").[74] The orchestration of different capabilities—expertise from different types of actors/stakeholders within the music industry—has transformed how music is created and the business of music orchestrated.

These shifts are also occurring within technology. Brian Arthur describes technology as a system whose elements are constantly updating their behavior based on their present situation. Technologies call forth or demand further technologies—whether data storage, languages, computational algorithms, machine learning, etc. These novel technologies, in turn, demand and supply yet further technologies. It follows that a novel technology is not just a one-time disruption to equilibrium, but a permanent, ongoing generator and demander of further technologies.[75]

Folks often cite Moore's law to characterize the inexorable drive of

---

73   Ibid., 85.

74   John Seabrook, *The Song Machine: Inside the Hit Factory* (New York: W.W. Norton, 2015).

75   W. Brian Arthur, *The Nature of Technology: What It Is and How It Evolves* (New York: Free Press, 2009).
     See also http://bigthink.com/the-nantucket-project/ray-kurzweil-the-six-epochs-of-technology-evolution,
     accessed January 18, 2016.

technology begetting—or affording the opportunities for different types of—technology. In 1965, Gordon Moore drew a graph of the number of components per integrated function on a silicon chip against time. He deduced that the number of transistors on a chip seemed to double every year and a half. This became the well-known Moore's law, indicating that the computing capacity would double every year and a half. Moore thought that his law would hit a limit when the size of each transistor reached 250 nanometers in diameter—but it hasn't, and the law continues chugging along quite nicely.[76] There are other patterns that underlie the *technology begets other technology* evolution.

Kryder's law states that the cost per performance of hard disk computer storage is rising exponentially at 40 percent per year. Cooper's law asserts that the number of possible simultaneous wireless communications has doubled every thirty months since 1895, when Marconi first broadcast. Edholm's law indicates that data rate of usage doubles every two years.[77] Wright's law states that the cost of a unit decreases as a function of the cumulative production.[78] And so on. These laws are largely independent of each other, but each reflects a core mechanism of technology evolution, their inexorable adaptation to changing needs—and value to capture. As Arthur explains it, "Existing technologies used in combination provide the possibilities of novel technologies: the potential supply of them. And human and technical needs create opportunity niches: the demand for them. As new technologies are brought in, new opportunities appear for further harnessing and further combinings. The whole bootstraps its way upward."[79]

How does this work?

---

76   Annie Sneed, "Moore's Law Keeps Going, Defying Expectations," Scientific American, May 19, 2015, http://www.scientificamerican.com/article/moore-s-law-keeps-going-defying-expectations/.

77   Ridley, *Evolution of Everything*. Also Georg Fischer, "A New View on Analogue-Digital-Balance with System Design," accessed January 18, 2016, http://www.wireless100gb.de/eumw2013/Fischer_EuMW2013.pdf.

78   "Wright's Law Edges Out Moore's Law," Spectrum.ieee.org, http://spectrum.ieee.org/tech-talk/at-work /test-and-measurement/wrights-law-edges-out-moores-law-in-predicting-technology-development, accessed July 15, 2017.

79   Arthur, *The Nature of Technology*: 176.

First: By Meeting a Specific Human or Market Need

In Chapter 1, we suggested that explosive growth has always come from meeting market breakdown, friction, and/or nonconsumption—variants of market needs to be met. Once we possess rocketry, we experience a need for space exploration. Once we have Facebook, we experience a need to connect everyone on the planet. Once we have the means to diagnose multidrug-resistant tuberculosis, we generate the organizational capability to tackle it. Novel technologies afford the opportunity to meet market needs that previously were deemed too expensive: economically, politically, and even organizationally. Technology evolution pulls along or demands the evolution of other supporting capabilities with it.

Second: By Recognizing That Technology Does Not Exist in Isolation

Every technology by its very existence sets up an opportunity for fulfilling its purpose more cheaply or efficiently. You need manufacturing capabilities to produce and distribute a technology, maintain it, and improve it. These, in turn, require their own bundles of technical capabilities to support them. IBM's aggressive restructuring around cognitive computing in early 2016 was based on the brilliant computational capabilities of Watson, known to many as the machine that won the *Jeopardy!* television game show, itself an evolution of its Deep Blue technology that gained notoriety through defeating Gary Kasparov, a world chess champion. Cognitive computing not only rests on a suite of adaptive machine learning algorithms but also requires enormous amounts of data to ingest, make sense of, and ensure its relevance to the set of tasks it has in front of it.[80]

The connected car is creating a set of ancillary needs—opportunity niches—for ever more precise data insight, particularly around changing conditions facing drivers, new types of insurance products, amount

---

80 See Pedro Domingos, *The Master Algorithm: How the Quest for the Ultimate Learning Machine Will Remake Our World* (New York: Basic Books, 2015).

of land needed in cities for parking, and battery storage companies, to mention but a few. And battery storage capabilities in turn set up further needs for battery distribution, transmission, and insight into usage.

Third: By Solving the Problems That Technology Causes

Technologies often cause problems—some intended, often not—that generate a new set of needs and opportunities for yet further solutions. Cognitive computing and the rise of machine learning have spawned concern over the implications for the global workforce as more and more jobs become automated. We are at an early stage of even beginning to see the contours of the types of possible risks of such a "singularity," whereby machine learning outpaces human capabilities. Much effort has been going into framing the possible effects on our workforce and how we organize for them. Increasing effort has been moving into understanding possible foreign policy, and security implications, not only in terms of the use of robotics for security or warfare but also for cascading risks such as the explosion of demographics—e.g., the enormous numbers of people under the age of twenty—in more volatile areas as a result of there being not enough jobs, or even the possibility of a "release valve" of so-called mid-tier jobs that machine learning could simply take away.[81]

Marc Andreessen once mentioned that software eats industries. He meant it in terms of new technologies tackling the friction present in existing industries, reducing that friction to near zero as a result of what technologies afford, and creating entirely new businesses as a result. We mean it in another, a complementary, way.

The calories expended in eating any industry go toward creating not only other technologies needed to digest the industry effectively but also through creating new opportunity niches that call forth even more technologies. In short, technology wants what every living system wants: to perpetuate itself. It is virtually impossible to turn the Internet off; it

---

81   See example of Robotics by Global Guerillas, January 2016. Also multiple discussions with Linton Wells (November 2015–June 2016).

affords itself new opportunities and requirements to adapt, and for market needs, value and opportunities to evolve.

> Technology wants what every living system wants:
> to perpetuate itself.

Fourth: By Taking Advantage of New Organizational Arrangements

As Eric Beinhocker reminds us, economic development is more than the growth of income. It is the appearance of an entire system of collaborative arrangements among people to meet specific desires. It has always emerged in response to folks seeking to exchange some unit of value (mechanism of exchange) for some thing they want (a product, service, or experience).[82] Over the centuries, it has changed form organically, with very little planning.

Karl Polanyi was a brilliant economic historian and philosopher. He wrote *The Great Transformation*, a magisterial book on the evolution of agrarian society to the Industrial Revolution. He described an evolution of behaviors, technologies, expectations, and policies that ended up creating a fundamentally new world, one nonplanned but emergent—the result of adaptive responses to changing environmental conditions.[83] In agrarian societies, a family was doing well if it could provide for itself; it grew what it could to feed itself with little left over to support anyone else. The harnessing of oxen, horses, wind, and water helped generate a bit more surplus energy, which allowed fields to be incrementally better, but not by much. There was a structural limit on how much a society could produce; it was constrained by the lack of surplus energy and capital to support much in terms of scale.

---

82   Beinhocker, *The Origin of Wealth.*
83   Karl Polanyi, *The Great Transformation: The Political and Economic Origins of Our Time* (Boston: Beacon Press, 1971).

The Industrial Revolution catalyzed a great transformation, not least of all in a seemingly inexhaustible supply of energy—in coal. Coal miners, unlike farmers, produced significantly more energy than they consumed. The rise of the steam engine was the catalyst for explosive growth in coal mining. It was a technology that called forth the development of other technologies: more machines to create more steam engines, larger roads to distribute the coal, larger ships to carry coal, which in turn required new skills to be able to make the larger ships and all the ancillary technologies and infrastructures they required. The evolution of surplus energy reflected an emergent, unplanned phenomena. It was also indispensable to the economic development of modern society.

Not to take this too far, but this is what the topic of platforms are in today's language. Much as surplus energy is indispensable to modern society, today's software platforms are indispensable to tomorrow's competitive environment. They are today's "surplus energy"—a capability that both calls for new technologies to be developed to meet shifting needs and amplifies the work of any person, or organization, who takes advantage of it. The line from the movie *The Gods Must Be Crazy* comes to the fore again: "Things that yesterday were unknown have today become indispensable." Both the evolution of surplus energy by industrialization and that afforded by platforms today are the result of emergent, unplanned phenomena.

And it is no different for business and how they organize themselves to capture new sources of value.

The point? *Value seeks forms that make it work.*

New sources of value select for organizational forms that enable them to get larger—to be captured and delivered. New business models represent these new organizational forms. They have evolved as logical ways to capture—and propagate—new sources of value. Business ecosystems are merely the logical extension of the new sources of value catalyzed by the shifts in our environment.

Each of the business ecosystems "selects" for how to capture (the changing types and sources of) value. They all have the same—harking back to Dawkins—"selfish" drive: to capture new sources of value. But how they do so differs. These differences rest in how they orchestrate different capabilities to capture and deliver that value.

Section Summary: What's Next for Business Ecosystems?

We don't know. There is a human tendency to seek answers to the question "What's next?"—to predict what is likely to happen. As we all know, prediction is as good as insight into the contours of a fog bank: you can see the fog that covers the details of what's behind it; seeing the contours within the bank provides, at least, a sense of the shape, though not the details, of what's to come. Details, we can't provide; contours, we can. We can begin to answer the "what, when, how, and why" questions of business ecosystems. It's those of the "where and who" that remain cloudy.

Of the former set of questions, business ecosystems are an adaptive response to capture new sources of value afforded by changes in technology, policy, demographics, and economics.

Wayne Gretzky, the legendary hockey player, is often quoted as having said, "I skate to where the puck is going to be, not where it has been." The same is true of organizations that recognize the way business ecosystems provide a new lens, much as the Hubble Telescope enabled us to see new stars, on new sources of value and opportunity. But more than that, their inherent focus on orchestrating capabilities across diverse actors in service to capture—and deliver—on that value reflects the blurring of industry lines so critical to being able to respond quickly and effectively to the opportunities that the new lens highlights.

Peter Drucker described that a business had a simple objective: to deliver value to its customer. As value changes, so too must the business. For him, then, how a business delivered value rested on a set of assumptions about what a business would and wouldn't do, could and couldn't do. It rested on assumptions around how to engage with customers, markets, and stakeholders in a way that they cared about—and valued. This is no more than what a business model is—a set of assumptions about where to focus and the mobilization of resources, capabilities, and calories to deliver value with speed and scale. An important difference exists between a business model and a competitive strategy. A business model describes how your business runs, whereas a competitive strategy explains how to do better than your rivals.

New business models powered by ecosystem-centric strategies reflect the inevitable adaptation to the complex interplay of technological changes, regulatory shifts, behavioral expectations, and demographic growth. You can't do it all. No one can. The shift in how value gets allocated as determined by the customer—discussed in the section "The Economics of Customer Experience"—has led to many of the firms, and people, we discussed rethinking how to bundle and unbundle their business models in ways that (a) reflect the reality of these changing economics and (b) require new ways to orchestrate the capabilities key to taking advantage of them.

We'll end with how we started.

Business ecosystems are inevitable organizational adaptations to capture new sources of value. As Deloitte crisply put it, "[They] create new ways to address fundamental needs and desires . . . The SIC-code, vertical-integration [business models] no longer work . . . They well captured the economic and business arrangements that transformed our lives in the 20th century."[84] But the logic of today has changed—with material consequences on how we make sense and take action on the new opportunities business ecosystems catalyze.

That business ecosystems are *the* key business model of today is not, we passionately believe, in question. What is in question is which one to use. We have attempted to describe what commonly underlies business ecosystems. We have also attempted to highlight what makes them

---

84 *Business Ecosystems Come of Age* (Westlake, TX: Deloitte University Press, 2015), accessed October 14, 2016, http://dupress.com/periodical/trends/business-trends-series/.

different. The reason? To provide you with a sense of the promise of what an ecosystem-centric business model can do for you, married with the pragmatics of how to figure out which kind is relevant for you and how to start engaging in it. No particular one is right for any particular business. A range of options exist, with trade-offs and implications for what you do and how you do it. But *do it* needs to be done.

Our Call to Action for You

Ask the new strategic questions. Change your unit of focus toward the ecosystem in which you—and your customers—are engaged. Engage your customers in new ways—in the ecosystem in which *they* care about. Double-down on your new 20 percent—and orchestrate the capabilities from others as you do so. Identify and capture both greater economic and social benefits. That's what tomorrow is about. That's what bold leaders are doing. That's what explosive growth is all about. Remember, it's all about identifying and capturing new sources of value in new ways. Otherwise, why bother?

Index

diabetes in sub-Saharan Africa, 72
Digital Transformation journey map,
     164–175
  outcomes, 48–50
Hogan, James, 116–17, 119–120, 123
hotel and home sharing services, 36–37,
     88, 101, 104–6
Hotels.com, 88
HSBC, 22
Hubble Telescope, 177, 200

I
IBM, 71, 115, 196
identity, 50–54
Industrial Revolution, 198–99
ING, 43–44
Innovation Portfolio journey map,
     179–185
  currencies model, 182
  data visualizations, 183–85
  diagram, 181
  ecosystem implications, 185
  execution plan, 185
  portfolio model, 182
  scenarios (possible worlds), 183
  shared value framework, 182
  Value Dynamics Model, 183
insurance. *See also* Digital Transformation
     journey map, 11, 41–43, 46–49,
     157, 159–160, 164, 173

J
jaws charts, 64–65, 104
JAXA, 88
Jeopardy! (TV show), 196
"jobs to be done" concept, 24, 107, 112,
     147
Johnson & Johnson, 70
journey maps, 163–187
  Consumer Engagement, 175–79
  Digital Transformation, 164–175
  Innovation Portfolio, 179–185

three generations of, 126–27
JPMorganChase, 114

K
Kasparov, Gary, 196
Kelly, Eamonn, 125
Kelly, Kevin, 28, 186
Kotler, Steven, 131
KPMG, 52
Kryder's law, 195

L
Lennon, John, 194
linked diagrams, 153
lock-in, 18, 81–83, 123
Lowe's, 42
Lyft, 37

M
magic (delight) touchpoints, 167
Malorodov, Alex, 95–96
Marconi, Guglielmo, 195
Mark (CEO of sporting goods firm),
     31–32, 58–59
market makers, 88, 101, 105
Martin Marietta Materials, 10
McCartney, Paul, 194
Merck, 70, 92, 125
Metropolitan Health, 15, 46–47, 49, 54,
     130, 158
micro loans, 22, 24–25
Microsoft, 10, 18–19, 71
Minimal Viable Product (MVP), 174
MIT, 129
mobile and telecommunications industry
  control points, 84
  health care, 48–49
  minutes as currency, 23–25
  traditional vs. OTT players, 63–65,
     79–81, 84–85, 104–5
  vertical integration model, 80–81

About the Authors

Ralph Welborn has spent over twenty-five years providing business and technology advisory services to both private and public sector organizations globally. He has held a variety of leadership positions, including CEO of Imaginatik, the market-leading innovation advisory and platform company; leader of IBM's Strategy & Transformation business in the Middle East and Africa; senior vice president at KPMG Consulting; and a cofounder of an e-commerce company. He has lived and worked around the world.

The common thread in much of Ralph's work is the design and deployment of new business models to capture explosive growth. His work draws from his experience in private and public sectors across industries and geographies.

In 2016 he received the European CEO award for technology companies. He has a bachelor's and master's degree in global public policy and a PhD in philosophy of science from Boston University. He lives in Boston with his family. He can be reached at ralph.topplebook@gmail.com.

Learn more about the models used in this book, including examples, at www.topplebook.com or by contacting Ralph.

Sajan Pillai is CEO of UST Global. He led the company's founding team of just twenty people in 1999. Eighteen years later, UST Global has grown to more than 18,000 employees operating in twenty-one countries around the globe.

His vision has made him a trusted partner to the national leaders of Mexico, Spain, United Kingdom, Saudi Arabia, Greece, Rwanda, Panama, Costa Rica, Russia, and Kazakhstan, and he is in discussions with many of them to establish digital and technology centers in their countries.

Sajan is as enthusiastic about nonprofit work as he is about business and serves on the boards of multiple nonprofit organizations, including the California Science Center, The Global Virus Network, Centro Fox in Mexico, and PEACE One Day Corporate Coalition.

Sajan holds an engineering degree from College of Engineering, Thiruvananthapuram, Kerala, India. Science, technology, community, and the arts inspire him as he engages in community initiatives in and around Orange County, California, where he lives with his family.